POWER in
NUMBERS

POWER in NUMBERS

UNITAID, Innovative Financing, and the Quest for Massive Good

Philippe Douste-Blazy &
Daniel Altman

WITH A PREFACE BY
BILL CLINTON

PublicAffairs
New York

Editorial production by *Marra*thon Production Services. www.marrathon.net

BOOK DESIGN BY JANE RAESE
Text set in 13-point Perpetua

Cataloging-in-Publication Data is available from the Library of Congress.
ISBN 978-1-58648-893-2

FIRST EDITION
10 9 8 7 6 5 4 3 2 1

To the people who have helped UNITAID,

and to the people whom UNITAID can help.

Thanks to Felix Marquardt for doing for us what he does best: bringing people together.

Contents

Preface

WITH EACH DAY, the world grows smaller. Our boundaries are blurred; our economic destinies are inseparable. Global financial crises expose how thoroughly entangled we have become — where, for better or worse, everything we do affects others both within and beyond our borders. Our fates are bound together, and, ultimately, it is our responsibility to utilize this widening interdependence for good, to maximize its transformative ability to empower the future.

Infectious diseases and their consequences have always been global phenomena. They are spread wherever people travel, presenting the world with a common challenge: to mitigate their damaging effects and, eventually, to eliminate them.

The task is enormous. More than thirty-three million people live with HIV/AIDS, 90 percent of them in developing nations. Every day, people die prematurely of HIV/AIDS and other diseases because they lack the provisions and treatments necessary for survival. These lives matter, and they can be saved. Doing so will require us to redefine our roles as global citizens. We can no longer ignore the plight of those who suffer thousands of miles away from our homes. Their lives affect ours, and we can affect theirs, strengthening our shared future.

Through *Power in Numbers,* Dr. Philippe Douste-Blazy and Daniel Altman offer a compelling vision of how humanity, even in the face of existing economic adversity, can stay on the path of progress. *Power in Numbers* describes how people of all incomes can help to address major global challenges — by donating small amounts to innovative financing mechanisms such as UNITAID.

Since 2006, UNITAID, which raises roughly $400 million per year to address health problems in developing nations, has partnered with the Clinton HIV/AIDS Initiative (CHAI). In just under four years, UNITAID has donated more than $193 million to CHAI, funds which have enabled us to reduce prices and expand access to pediatric and second-line HIV/AIDS treatments all over the world. By 2009, our Pediatrics Project helped initiate treatment for nearly 220,000 children, about two-thirds of all the children in developing nations receiving pediatric AIDS medicine. And our high-volume purchases have reduced the medicine's cost by 90 percent. We have also been able to reduce the costs and provide more second-line antiretroviral drugs to low-income countries, enabling many more families to lead productive lives and contribute to their communities.

Without the millions of people who have supported programs such as UNITAID, our work would not have been possible. *Power in Numbers* shows how partnerships, large and small, have the ability to transform inequity and poverty into growth and renewal.

As global citizens, our hope for progress is inextricably linked to the partnerships, some of them reaching across the public and private sectors, championed by *Power in Numbers*.

The authors show us how we can build an integrated global society of shared responsibilities, shared opportunities, and shared values. And because we can, we must. I am pleased to join Philippe Douste-Blazy and Daniel Altman in encouraging you to participate in this vital mission in whatever way you can, for as little as two dollars.

President Bill Clinton

Chapter 1

A Gap That Must Be Closed

Our true nationality is mankind.

— H. G. WELLS

IN 1994, in a hospital in Côte d'Ivoire, forty children lay dying in a cramped hospital ward. Black flies circled the room, landing with impunity on the bodies of the tiny human beings so beaten down by disease that they could do nothing to shoo them away. The hospital offered no treatment to lessen the agony of the children's death throes. When a doctor was asked why no one attended to the children, he said, "They have AIDS, leave them." The children were being left to die. There was no medicine to treat them, so the doctors had abandoned them to their fate. Within months, all forty lives would be lost.

These children did nothing to deserve this destiny. The simple fact of their birth in a poor country, overwhelmed by a seemingly uncontrollable disease, doomed them to this early and undignified end. Their deaths would go unnoticed by much of the world; they were nothing more than a sad side effect of an epidemic that was taking on surreal proportions in a faraway land.

Yet that epidemic — and indeed rampant disease of any kind — is not a remote event, even when it pervades a country that is very far away. The effects are real and can be felt around the world. A sick country cannot be a successful country, either socially or economically. Disease breaks down the family, stealing mothers and fathers or burdening them with the sorrow of losing a child. It carves the heart out of the workforce, cutting down able-bodied men and women in their prime of life. It foments instability as citizens react against helpless governments and countries look across their borders to replace the crops they could not harvest, the minerals they could not mine, and even the soldiers they could not recruit.

The epidemics that rage across the world's tropical zones have not just robbed the worst-affected countries of their future. They have also taken new markets away from businesses in wealthier nations and fuelled regional crises that threaten to pull those nations' governments into crucibles of conflict. Nor is disease a one-off event or a containable catastrophe; if disease takes root, it can be an ongoing scourge, dwarfing the devastating effects of other disasters. Consider the death tolls of these humanitarian tragedies in recent history:

Sichuan earthquake (2008)	68,000
Asian tsunami (2004–2005)	220,000

Iraq war (2002–2006)	600,000
Rwandan genocide (1994)	800,000
Cambodian genocide (1975–1979)	1,700,000
HIV/AIDS, malaria, and tuberculosis in developing countries	more than 3,000,000 every year

Clearly, all of these were horrible catastrophes. But unlike earthquakes and tsunamis, the deaths from the three major epidemics are preventable. In wealthy countries, HIV/AIDS has virtually become a chronic disease; patients can expect to live for decades after their diagnosis. Tuberculosis and malaria are completely curable in the vast majority of cases. Saving the millions of lives lost to these epidemics doesn't require troop deployments, economic sanctions, or difficult diplomacy. Yet while we rush to the aid of people hit by natural disasters and loudly lament genocides, we still allow those millions of lives lost to epidemics — those millions of people like us — to vanish forever.

The epidemics have laid down the gauntlet for the citizens of the world. Because the diseases are treatable, it is a failure of human will that we do not yet treat all the people who suffer from them. We could, but we don't. Why should those children doomed to die among the flies be less deserving than any others? At the heart of the notion of human solidarity is a question of equality: Will we stand by and leave more children to die, or will we stand up for their rights as human beings the way we stand up to protect those in our own country?

SOLIDARITY IS a complicated topic. Its origins can be philosophical and religious; its effects can be political and economic. Within countries, solidarity can be hard to come by, or it can be routine, dutiful, and even institutionalized. In wealthy countries, for example, the state often collects taxes from the haves to provide money, food, housing, education, childcare, and medical treatments to the have-nots. In these countries, guaranteeing a basic standard of survival for every citizen is the government's responsibility, and the more fortunate are usually willing to share — up to a point — with the less fortunate in their society.

When that magnanimity tries to cross borders, however, it can peter out quickly. Budgets for foreign aid are notoriously contentious in the political arena, and even the wealthiest nations give just a tiny fraction of their incomes to help the poor in other countries. Since 1970, the United Nations has asked wealthy countries to raise their annual development aid to 0.7 percent of gross domestic product — a minuscule percentage, but an enormous increase with respect to current levels for most of them. Even in 2005, when the European Union agreed to a timetable to reach the 0.7 percent goal, the world's three biggest economies — then the United States, Japan, and Germany — gave only 0.22, 0.28, and 0.35 percent, respectively. And today, the world's wealthy countries still give far more so that other countries can buy guns than they do so that other countries can buy medicines.

And today, many of the world's wealthy countries, and even rich citizens of poor countries, might shy away from further aid for many reasons. The problems of the poor may seem distant, and it is not easy to figure out which kind of aid is appropriate. It is difficult to argue that a Spaniard should pay to make sure that a Laotian has a decent house to live in. How poor should the Laotian be to deserve the house? How rich should the Spaniard be to feel an obligation to pay? How nice should the house be? The argument about the principle — whether the Spaniard feels any solidarity with the Laotian — can easily get lost in the details.

In the case of epidemics, however, the argument becomes clearer: Disease is often a matter of life and death. Without treatment, the sick will die. In most cases, they became infected through no fault of their own; ignorance, poor public health, environmental conditions, and even the climate in which they live can contribute to their illness. To declare that they should be left to suffer the consequences of these factors, virtually all of which were beyond their control, is close to saying that they should never have been born in the first place. Anyone who possesses the merest feeling of solidarity with his or her fellow human beings will find that idea detestable.

But feeling sympathetic and being able to express that sympathy in a way that is measured and targeted are not the same thing. Some of us are simply overwhelmed by the scale of the challenge. Who, individually, can imagine bringing the effects of malaria to a halt? The problem seems too big for a single person's actions to make any difference. Indeed, the problem is so huge that no one country affected by disease can solve it on its own, given the political and economic realities that the world now faces. That is exactly why the mobilization of individuals around the world is so vitally important. There is power in numbers.

Now we have a mechanism, and a choice. Every time each of us buys an airline ticket from a website such as Orbitz or Opodo, and soon every time we stay in one of thousands of hotels such as Accor's Sofitel or Novotel, or when we book a vacation with American Express, we can participate directly in the fight against the big three infectious diseases. When we pay for our travel, we have the option to make a small donation — a voluntary contribution of as little as two dollars — to show our solidarity and save lives in the developing world. In an instant, each of us can make a small but significant gesture of support and participate in the biggest global campaign ever to bring people out of the misery and poverty inflicted by disease.

EPIDEMICS RAGE throughout the world's tropical zones, occasionally becoming the subjects of intense attention from the international media, as the ebola virus did in the 1990s and dengue fever did in the 2000s. But no single infectious disease causes as many deaths in developing countries (or indeed in the world as a whole) as each of the three big epidemics: AIDS, tuberculosis, and malaria. In 2004, the last year for which statistics were available at the time of this writing, these three diseases caused one in eight of all deaths, from any cause, in low-income countries.

Moreover, the three diseases interact. Cases of latent tuberculosis, where the germ remains inactive in the body, are common in areas where people are infected with the disease. The overall prevalence rate could be as high as 21 percent in China, for example, compared with about 4 percent in the United States. Many of these cases may never become active. But in people with HIV, latent tuberculosis is much more likely to explode into a full-blown infection, and those infections tend to be much more severe than in people without HIV. Full-blown tuberculosis is more infectious, meaning that one epidemic can directly feed into another one. And people without latent tuberculosis are also much more susceptible to being infected if they already have HIV.

The suppression of the immune system caused by HIV/AIDS also makes it harder for people to fight off malaria. Malaria may also make HIV worse. Patients with both diseases tend to have more HIV in their bloodstreams than those with HIV alone. Medical research suggests that when the body creates antigens to fight malaria, it actually helps HIV to replicate.

Not surprisingly, patients in the developing world — especially in the tropical zones of Latin America, the Caribbean, Africa, and Southeast Asia — are often diagnosed with combinations of all three of the diseases, which may all be present in varying strengths. Because of their interactions and the fact that the infected populations overlap so much, it makes sense to fight the three diseases together.

HIV/AIDS, tuberculosis, and malaria don't kill as many people around the world as heart disease and cancer. Worldwide, the mortality rate for heart disease and cancer is five times higher than the rate for AIDS, tuberculosis, and malaria. But heart disease and cancers are not infectious, like HIV and tuberculosis, and their victims are rarely children. By contrast, AIDS, tuberculosis, and malaria kill millions of young adults, children, and babies every year — people who haven't had the chance to live long or full lives. Stopping AIDS, tuberculosis, and malaria doesn't just add a few years of life; it adds a lifetime.

This is especially true for AIDS, because thousands of children are born HIV-positive every year, like a seven-year-old girl who came to a hospital in Burkina Faso in 2006 looking terribly thin, her mother in tears and the doctors convinced that the girl would soon die. A year and a half later, however, she was back in the hospital for a checkup, healthy and practically unrecognizable, smiling, giggling, and holding a drawing she'd made for the doctors there. Three-way antiretroviral therapy had saved her life. Instead of dying at seven, she can expect to live, most likely, to the age of sixty-two — an addition of fifty-five years of life, giving her the chance to have children and grandchildren, pursue her ambitions, and contribute to her country's future.

Even this victory over disease seems somewhat hollow, though, when one realizes that the girl was saved only on the second opportunity. She was born with HIV because her mother has the virus, but today's therapies can stop HIV from being transmitted from mother to child, too. Had the girl's mother been treated, the girl could have been born healthy.

Protecting children is especially important for economic growth in the developing world. When more children live, mothers trying to build a family have to go through fewer arduous and perhaps even dangerous pregnancies. When more children live, mothers and fathers are more likely to invest time and resources in that child's health and education. When more children live, it becomes more likely that each generation in a developing country will be better off than the generation that came before.

And saving a child doesn't only make a difference to that child, her family, and her country. It also has very real benefits for the rest of the world. For example, consider what happens when a child is saved from deadly malaria in Guatemala, where people living in three-quarters of the country are at risk of infection. Per capita income in Guatemala was about $2,800 per year in 2008, and imports of goods and services were about $1,000 per capita. Guatemala is one of the most unequal countries in the world, though, and a child who might have fallen victim to malaria is likely to be poor and living in a rural area. So, if the child lives to adulthood, his or her income may be no more than $1,000 per year. She may spend about $300 of that money on imports, in line with the national average, because Guatemala does not have much homegrown industry and must import both food and fuel. Now, a third of Guatemala's imports came from the United States in 2008. So, if that proportion holds in the future, the child will spend $100 per year on imports from the United States, over a working life of perhaps forty years. That's $4,000 in imports from the United States for the price of protecting one child against malaria. How much does that protection cost? About $6 for a full course of the most effective drugs against the disease, and another $10 for a top-quality insecticide-treated bednet to stop infection at night. From 1969 to 2009, Warren Buffett, perhaps the world's most famous investor, managed to multiply his wealth about two hundred fifty times over, adjusted for inflation. He received the same rate of return that a $16 investment in a poor person in Guatemala would generate for the American economy.

Lost economic activity is only one of the costs of disease. Epidemics also cause pain, fear, and other forms of psychological distress. They make it harder to keep family units together and raise children. They lead to aberrant and cruel behavior, such as the rape of virgin girls, a practice that some men in African countries erroneously believe will protect against or even cure HIV. They can also lead to violent upheaval. As early as 1987, a report by the Central Intelligence Agency discussed the danger that HIV would exacerbate conflict in sub-Saharan Africa. One academic study using data from developing countries showed that the prevalence of AIDS was strongly associated with worse levels of civil conflict and abuses of human rights. In a multistage statistical model, Susan Peterson of the College of William and Mary and Stephen Shellman of the University of Georgia demonstrated that epidemics pulled down incomes, educational attainment, and the quality of political institutions in these countries, which in turn hurt the level of security. Other recent research by Andrew Price-Smith of Colorado College suggests that the erosion of public health by any epidemic can distort demographics (for example, by removing caregivers from families and productive workers from the labor force), weaken governments, and reduce the state's ability to take care of its people, all of which can in turn lead to conflict. Even if that conflict occurs in faraway, poor countries, it can drive up prices for the commodities they produce, disrupt the operations of companies based in rich countries that do business overseas, and involve foreign governments in costly interventions.

This situation is repeated across the developing world. Most poor countries cannot afford to import all the medical products they need from rich countries, but they cannot produce them at home, either. Their leaders know that HIV/AIDS, malaria, and tuberculosis are standing in the way of their growth and development, and of their participation in the global economy. As Tandja Mamadou, Niger's president, said in 2004, "Our number one problem is AIDS and its attendant diseases, because a lot of the schoolteachers, nurses, and engineers are infected, and a lot of the youth is infected, and it's absolutely impossible to see the growth of a country without youth." When the leaders and ministers of French-speaking countries in Africa gathered in 2006 in Bamako, Mali, the conclusion was the same: They needed donations of treatments for AIDS if they were going to see development. It was simply a precondition for escaping from the abject poverty that blanketed their lands. Aid agencies could talk about teaching someone to fish instead of giving them fish to eat, but if a person was too sick to fish it made little difference. Medical care was the absolute priority; learning to fish could come later.

Treatments for HIV/AIDS, tuberculosis, and malaria are not only attainable but also effective. Just as that seven-year-old girl was saved from the ravages of AIDS by three-way therapy, tuberculosis patients around the world are being helped by medicines that can kill even drug-resistant bacteria, and millions of people are staving off infection by malaria-carrying mosquitoes by sleeping under specially designed bednets. Meanwhile, the search continues for new vaccines and better ways of delivering the old treatments.

From a medical perspective, this is a time of great hope. One step is missing, however: bringing the treatments from the laboratories and testing clinics into the homes of hundreds of millions of people, many of whom live in tiny communities scattered along remote dirt roads in some of the hottest and muggiest places on earth. It is an enormous challenge, requiring not just money but strategic thinking and expertise. So far, it has not been met.

Is THE WORLD now finally ready to meet this challenge? One facile objection to giving more money to developing countries is that they already receive billions of dollars every year in aid from foreign governments and nongovernmental organizations. Isn't there already enough money to stop these diseases, if the treatments are available? The answer is simply no. In 2007, wealthy countries committed $118 billion in direct aid to the developing world, but only $5.3 billion was earmarked for health programs and just $2.2 billion for nongovernmental organizations, some of which also delivered health services. At the beginning of 2007, more than five million HIV-positive people who needed antiretroviral treatment but were not receiving it lived in developing countries. To treat all of them every day for a year with the most basic regimen of drugs would have required raising aid for health by 20 to 30 percent — and that was just for one disease. To give them the latest generation of antiretroviral treatments, health-related aid would have had to more than double.

Clearly, the money is not there. Even when governments in developing countries do spend money on public health, it can be difficult for them to invest effectively. If they buy medical treatments only occasionally as individual purchasers, they cannot negotiate prices as low as the ones they might obtain if they were to bargain with pharmaceutical companies as a group. They might also miss out on discounts that can be available under long-term contracts, because their spending is dependent on annually renewable installments of aid money that they can't always count on. Unsurprisingly, commitments of aid started to drop just as the recent global economic crisis began. The United States and other major economies entered a recession in 2007, and aid that year fell by one hundred million dollars compared with 2006.

The old models for aid simply have not accomplished enough. But the diseases won't wait for aid budgets to catch up. They can become stronger while treatment is sparse, evolving into new strains that can't be killed with existing treatments and that infect more people, making the contagion harder to contain. To turn the corner and stop the spread of these diseases, in line with the great successes of the past such as the virtual elimination of smallpox, polio, and measles, the scale of treatment must make a quantum leap. But how?

That was the question occupying the minds of two heads of state — one a patrician politician with an air of seniority who had bided his time for decades on the center-right until he became the inevitable choice of his country's majority, the other a street-fighting labor boss who had somehow ridden a grassroots movement into his nation's highest office without resorting to demagoguery — as they shared a private toast during an official visit in 2005. In just four years, a program they helped to start would raise more than $1.4 billion to fight disease. The story of that program, however, began several years earlier, in a mountainous Mexican city thousands of miles away from most of the people whose lives it would someday save.

Chapter 2

The Story of UNITAID

. . . each man must invent his own path.
— JEAN-PAUL SARTRE

AS TOLD BY PHILIPPE DOUSTE-BLAZY:

Most presidents like to leave a legacy when they step down from the highest office in the land. French presidents are no different. In France, there has been a tendency to look to large architectural expressions, such as the four gigantic towers of the National Library constructed in the waning years of François Mitterrand's administration. As Jacques Chirac settled into his second term as president, he undoubtedly realized that he would be seventy-four at its conclusion. He had already begun to think about ways to cement his status as a great leader. But instead of towering buildings, he chose the Millennium Development Goals as his challenge.

The goals had been set in 2000 as part of a new focus by the United Nations and other international agencies on fighting the enemies of human development — hunger, disease, and poverty — around the world. The goals sought to cut global poverty in half by 2015 and also to guarantee primary education, promote gender equality, improve mothers' and children's health, protect the environment, and fight HIV/AIDS, malaria, and tuberculosis. They were ambitious targets, and from the start researchers saw that the money needed to reach them simply was not there. To achieve all the goals, worldwide development aid would have had to rise overnight by about half, or fifty billion dollars a year.

Clearly, there was a need for new ways to finance programs that could reliably improve human and economic development in poor countries. In 2002, the United Nations convened a special meeting in Monterrey, Mexico, to address the issue. More than fifty heads of state attended, including Chirac. At the meeting, Chirac encouraged his fellow heads of state to look more seriously at the idea of an international tax on financial transactions, an idea that had originally been proposed by the late Nobel laureate economist James Tobin as a way to slow speculation in the currency markets. At the time, the response was lukewarm. The reports generated by the conference identified the gap in financing but offered little in the way of concrete action to close it. Ultimately, Chirac decided that he and his government would take the next step.

In November 2003, he asked Jean-Pierre Landau, a lifetime civil servant then working as France's director on the board of the European Bank for Reconstruction and Development, to head an investigation into a growing set of fund-raising and financial devices that had begun to be known as "innovative financing." The focus of the study, whose authors would include other French civil servants, the famed Oxford economist Sir

Tony Atkinson, executives of huge corporations including Areva and Suez, and the head of research at the charity Oxfam, was the idea that some kind of international tax should be levied to convert the prosperity generated by globalization into an engine for change in poor countries.

For a conservative politician, this was quite a departure. Not only was Chirac backing a system of tax-and-transfer redistribution; it was a system of redistribution whose millions of beneficiaries might not even live in the same countries as the people paying the tax.

In March 2004, Chirac called a meeting with two top advisers at his residence, the Elysée Palace, to discuss the result of Landau's research. I was invited because I was the minister of health and had always been involved in the cause of international development.

The atmosphere was intimate, with only five people in the room. For a head of state even to be considering the idea of an international tax was a sensitive matter. The Landau Report was bold in other ways, as well. It ran to almost one hundred pages, and it considered a slew of options for the tax: credit card payments, purchases of securities, foreign exchange transactions, arms sales, corporate profits, environmental markets, shipping, and air transport. It weighed the pluses and minuses of taxes versus voluntary contributions, and it even considered the idea of a global lottery. But many of the options had serious problems. Taxes on corporate profits or purchases of securities — this was long before the financial crisis that struck in 2008 — would have run into severe political opposition in France and elsewhere. Environmental markets were already a difficult topic, given the lack of a worldwide consensus on cutting harmful emissions.

So, as we discussed the options, we eventually went back to the motivation for the original idea: the unequal distribution of the prosperity generated by globalization. The gap between rich and poor people was becoming more and more important because of globalization; the rich were simply better able to take advantage of the opportunities that globalization created because of their superior education, wealth, and connections. The global elite, symbolic of the era of globalization, could often be found above thirty thousand feet in business class. Plane tickets were a perfect symbol of globalization. We thought that a tax on air travel was the easiest tax to implement because there were already so many taxes on plane tickets. Airline tickets were also a discretionary purchase for most consumers: Flying was not an essential part of the basket of goods and services needed to survive. By definition, therefore, this tax would not fall on those who could not afford to pay it: A man or a woman who can buy a plane ticket can pay an additional one dollar or two dollars — less than the cost of a cup of coffee at the airport — rather painlessly. So Chirac's group settled on the idea of an additional tiny tax on plane tickets around the world, collecting a dollar or two — perhaps more for business or first-class tickets — from each one of the billions of tickets sold every year. Given that the tax would work out to be less than 1 percent of the purchase price of a ticket, and the fact that ticket prices changed all the time in ways that weren't always transparent to consumers, the burden on the air travel market would be negligible. All in all, it was a nice idea — that no one had a specific plan for. I backed it at once. But I was the health minister, and it had little to do with my official duties. Someone else would have to implement it.

News of the report circulated during a conference on development held by Chirac and the Brazilian president, Luiz Inácio Lula da Silva, at the United Nations in September 2004. Even Chirac himself called the ideas in the report "radically new." The media covered the conference and created a buzz of interest, but it died down until the meeting of the World Economic Forum in January 2005. There, in Davos, Switzerland, we spoke about the possibility of an international tax again. Chirac, Lula, and Ricardo Lagos, the president of Chile, created an association called Action Against Hunger and Poverty with a call to develop and further investigate innovative financing.

This time Chirac mentioned the possibility of taxes on financial transactions, airline tickets, and a few of the other options in the Landau Report. It didn't take long for the word "taxes" to spur a reaction. Tony Fratto, a spokesman for the Treasury in Washington, put the American administration's position bluntly: "The United States is not inclined to support international taxation schemes."

For the next two months, nothing happened. But in late March 2005, we brought up the idea again, this time focusing on the airline tax as a starting point for the program. Again, the reaction was immediate. Right away we received a barrage of complaints from the entire aeronautical industry, saying, "Why us? Why not the trains? Why not cars? You're going to kill us. You are against tourism." The tax was misrepresented and vilified, and in France it was presented as an idea that would bring tourism to a standstill. (This was a particularly ignorant reaction: Because we could not apply the tax outside France, tourists from abroad wouldn't be paying it, and, anyway, many of them did not arrive by air. Two-thirds of the hotel nights purchased in France are paid for by French people! But this reaction was typical of the hysteria that the word *tax* could generate.) The proposal had been shouted down once more, and it slipped quietly off the agenda.

In June 2005, it was my turn to try and make the tiny tax a reality. I was made foreign minister in the new government chosen by Chirac. This position gave me the chance to raise the profile of the innovative financing project, and I personally took it on. My first trip overseas as foreign minister was to be to the United States. I called the French ambassador in Washington to arrange the itinerary. As was customary, because foreign visits acquire a routine quality, the ambassador asked me, "Minister, you want to come to the United States? What agenda shall I organize for you?"

I said, "Well, first I want to see my counterpart, Condoleezza Rice, and then I'm going to give some medals to some veterans, as every French foreign minister has done for fifty years. But then I want to have an appointment with the world's best living politician."

"Who is he?"

"Bill Clinton."

And so, after I crossed the Atlantic, I traveled with the French ambassador up to Chappaqua, a picturesque suburb in Westchester, outside New York City, to be greeted by Bill Clinton, who was dressed in jeans and a yellow Lacoste shirt, with a mug of coffee in his right hand. The previous night, while I had been en route from Paris, the decision was made as to which city would host the 2012 Olympics. The final contest was between Paris and London. Clinton's first words to me were, "It's London."

But things picked up from there. We spent two hours together — talking about Israel, Palestine, and Europe, then about the health care systems in the United States and in France — and then I told Clinton that I had a particular question that I wanted to put to him, and I described the idea for the air travel tax. I explained that it would, if implemented, potentially generate two, three, four, five, even six hundred million dollars every year. "What," I wanted to know from Clinton, "do you think I should do with the money?"

Just two months later, Clinton would convene the first of his Clinton Global Initiatives, and the meeting would raise two-and-a-half billion dollars in pledges. Philanthropy was a topic that truly motivated him, and he had an answer to my question: "I know what you have to do. You have to do, on a big scale, what I do with my foundation. You have to work on drugs to fight HIV/AIDS, malaria, and tuberculosis." I told him I wanted to work on them — the sixth Millennium

Development Goal, as well as the parts of the fourth and fifth goals concerning child mortality and mothers' health. But Clinton pushed for more: "You have to say to the drug companies, I'm giving you money, not for one year but for several years, for example, three hundred million dollars per year for five years. How much do you agree to decrease the price?" That was the genesis of the idea that became UNITAID. I said, "Thank you very much, Mr. President. I knew that I could find an idea here."

It is rare to find a head of state who is interested in the health of developing countries. I'm a doctor, and I was twice minister of health, so I was always interested in the topic. But heads of state are more typically lawyers or businessmen, or products of local political machines whose sensibility and experience may not include the world's more disadvantaged places. Yet Clinton has always had an awareness of the bigger picture. During his presidency, he championed unrestricted access to the United States for exporters in democratic African countries as a spark for economic growth on an impoverished continent. Now, in our meeting, he had helped me to formulate another way in which the developed world might lend a hand to disadvantaged nations.

THE MEETING with Bill Clinton left me energized and eager to move forward. I had known before that I wanted to help the world reach the Millennium Development Goals, to use an airline ticket tax to raise the money, and to focus on the goals related to health. But Clinton had given me the direction I needed to make a difference. To our innovative financing, we were going to add innovative spending.

The next month, Lula was Chirac's guest at the festivities for July 14, the French national holiday. The friendship between the two men, who could not have been more different in their backgrounds or their political views, had grown through their common interest in development. At one o'clock in the afternoon, Chirac had a press conference on television with some of France's top journalists. During the broadcast, I joined Lula in Chirac's office at the Elysée Palace.

We quickly got into an animated discussion of the airline tax. Then Chirac came back to his office after the broadcast looking very pleased, and we had an aperitif together. Chirac said to Lula, "I picked a doctor as foreign minister because the world is sick," and they both had a good laugh. They were the presidents, after all. But I took advantage as they were laughing by saying, "You've both spoken about an airline ticket tax, but what is it for?"

In the past, they had spoken only broadly about the Millennium Development Goals and the idea of a grand global redistribution of wealth. But Lula had a specific answer as we shared that aperitif: the fight against hunger. Then, Chirac suggested the fight against AIDS. I pointed out that the two of them had entirely different answers, at which point they agreed to let me decide on their joint behalf. So at last I had the chance to combine the idea with Clinton's advice. I took charge of the project and decided to create the international facility for drug purchases, whose acronym worked out to FIAM in French. It wasn't a pretty name, but the name wouldn't last long.

EVEN THOUGH I had a fairly clear idea of how I wanted the program to work, whenever the idea for the tax came under public scrutiny it generated a lot of instinctive and often irrational hostility. But that's taxes for you. A lot of skepticism was expressed about Chirac and about me, even among the other ministers in the French cabinet. The project needed credibility to keep moving forward.

In September 2005, I called Lee Jong-wook, the director-general of the World Health Organization, to ask if we could have dinner in the Quai d'Orsay, where the offices of the foreign ministry are located. I did the same thing with Peter Piot, the head of the Joint United Nations Program on HIV and AIDS. After that, I called Ira Magaziner, the chairman of the Clinton Foundation, and Richard Feacham, who was then the Executive Director of the Global Fund to Fight AIDS, Tuberculosis and Malaria. When I had these representatives of some of the most important health-related organizations in the world sitting around the same table, I said to them, "I would like to set up a laboratory for innovative financing using a solidarity contribution on plane tickets." The response was positive and unanimous, and with this consensus, at the end of the dinner, the landscape for global health had already begun to change.

Together, these experts wrote a communiqué that advisers of ministers around the world would see, endorsing the airline ticket tax. But it was not enough for a group of smart and well-meaning people to say that we had a good idea. To make the idea a reality, we would have to gain political traction as well. For this, I had to be patient. In the fall of 2005, Chirac was preoccupied by a variety of issues — the aftermath of France's "no" vote on the European Constitution, the reconstruction of the French alliance with the United Kingdom, the riots by young jobless people around Paris — and I had to wait for the right moment to bring the airline tax back to the center of his attention.

My first opportunity to see the president face-to-face, without advisers, came at the European Council meeting in December 2005 in Brussels. There, the leader of each member of the European Union and his or her minister of foreign affairs were given one car to share while traveling from their hotel to the council chamber. The same was true for Tony Blair, for Angela Merkel, for every head of state. The cars were reinforced for security, with glass between the front and back seats, and no telephone. Between the hotel and the European Council chamber, Chirac and I had twenty minutes when nothing could interrupt us.

Twenty minutes there and back each day for two days amounted to eighty minutes with the president with no schedule and no agenda — priceless. As soon as I could, I turned the conversation to the tax on plane tickets. I reminded Chirac of the work that I had been doing and told him for the first time about the memo that the experts had compiled. In general, it's very difficult to give a memo directly to a head of state because you have at least two hands of his advisers reaching for it. But there, in the car, there were no such obstacles; I could simply hand him the memo with the idea for the international facility to purchase drugs. And he said to me, "It's a good idea. Perfect, Philippe. Move forward."

That was the crucial moment. I knew it two days later, when I saw an adviser to Chirac who had been completely neutral about the project since its inception. He said to me, "Oh, it's a fantastic idea, Mr. Minister!" It was obvious that the president had told him, "You have to do it." The follow-up was guaranteed. This is how politics works: The power of the presidency is such that when it is known that the president supports something, a perceptible shift of resources and willingness begins to occur. It isn't enough for the president merely to say something — as he had before — because a head of state has two hundred things to do every day. When he tells an adviser to follow up, however, that thing, whatever it is, will happen.

CREATING AN administrative motor from scratch for a project like this one would be difficult. I needed help, and so I called upon Jean Dussourd, a graduate of the National School of Administration, which trains the vast majority of France's top civil servants. From our encounters earlier in my career, I knew that he possessed the three characteristics I was seeking: He was a bulldozer, he was rigorous, and he loved a challenge. When I contacted him, he had just finished working as the deputy special representative for the secretary-general of the United Nations in Kosovo — not exactly an easy job.

When I told him that one of Chirac's most powerful advisers had declared the project a "good idea," he perked right up. Then I told him, "Jean, I know you. I am going to give you the most important thing you're going to do in your life. We are alone, except for the president, but it's enough to get things done. You have to organize this with other countries because we need not a French project but a multilateral project. The most difficult thing to do is to organize immediate action with other countries."

I asked Nicolas Sarkozy, then the minister of interior, to re-hire Dussourd and loan him to me at the foreign ministry. He arrived in January 2006, and I put him together with Philippe Duneton, who had been one of my directors when I was minister of health in 2004 and 2005. Duneton was a specialist in drugs and medicines who had gone to Africa with me to talk to the people working on the ground — UNICEF, the WHO, and nongovernmental organizations — about how the public health system could fight against AIDS, tuberculosis, and malaria. He seemed impassioned by the work and knew the terrain. This duo was the key to the project's success.

Our task was simple: to convince as many countries as possible to institute the airline ticket tax. We would take care of collecting the taxes and allocating its revenues, but we needed the politicians to pass the laws first. France was already on board, but France could not go it alone.

Dussourd began canvassing for the project, speaking to

governments around the world. He organized a big meeting, our first meeting, called the Leading Group for Innovative Financing for Development, in February 2006, and representatives of forty-four countries — many of them African — came to Paris. At the meeting, we discussed many types of innovative financing mechanisms with varying levels of government involvement: taxes, bond guarantees, private-sector fund-raising, and the like.

Behind the scenes, we started meeting with the individual countries' representatives. First we met the Norwegian administration, which has been interested in global health issues for a long time, and we came away with a positive response. Then we met the Brazilian administration, which was even easier, because Lula had already pledged his support in principle to Chirac in the fight against hunger and poverty. We also sat down with members of the United Kingdom's Department for International Development, which turned out to be extremely important because it led to a meeting with Gordon Brown.

At that time, Brown was the United Kingdom's chancellor of the exchequer, a position equivalent to finance minister whose power is second only to the prime minister's. He was already launching an innovative financing initiative called the International Finance Facility for Immunization (IFFIm), which had a clever way of raising money: using the financial markets to convert future donations by governments into money available for immediate spending on vaccines. To do this, IFFIm issued bonds on the regular financial markets with competitive interest rates. The bonds were backed by IFFIm's member governments, which promised to pay the interest and principal over the course of many years. But investors bought the bonds right away, putting vast sums of money at IFFIm's immediate disposal.

At that point, IFFIm transferred the money to the Global Alliances for Vaccines and Immunization (GAVI), which delivered the treatments on the ground. Receiving such a big chunk of money meant that GAVI could treat people sooner and, just as important, it could buy vaccines in huge volumes at lower prices. All this was accomplished by simply trading a long stream of official donations for the up-front revenue that came from selling bonds. In IFFIm's first year, it raised one billion dollars and immunized 120 million children — a stunning result. And so it was little surprise to us when Gordon Brown said, "Okay, I'm going to join, but I want France to give money to IFFIm."

Afterward, I had a meeting with Chirac. "Please, Mr. President," I said, "we have to exchange some of the money from the French tax with IFFIm. If we give 10 percent of the revenue to IFFIm, in return Gordon Brown is going to enter the project with us." With Chirac's permission and the help of his finance minister, that's exactly what we did.

WHILE DUSSOURD AND DUNETON were lobbying more countries to join us, I began to plan our public relations strategy. We were going to launch the tax in France in September

2006, and I wanted to start explaining the project in the press, on television, and on the radio. We started our own lobbying campaign, asking different popular personalities in France to endorse the tax. One of them was Emmanuel Jayr, a former radio DJ who at just thirty years old had become director of NRJ, one of the top radio stations in France. Jayr was already a big fan of the project, and I told him that I was going to try to convince Sepp Blatter, the head of the International Federation of Football Associations (FIFA), to publicize the project at the World Cup coming up that summer.

"You want to sell this to Blatter with the name FIAM?" he said. "What's FIAM?" When I explained what the acronym stood for, he said, "You're crazy. People won't get that. No."

I didn't know what to say. We had no money to hire consultants in rebranding, and our expertise in this area in the foreign ministry was limited: A couple of middle-aged civil servants were not the right people to come up with the hook for a huge marketing push. Jayr told me to give him "two or three days."

Three days later, he returned. "I have the name: *Tous Unis pour Aider* (Everyone United to Help)."

"That's too long," I said.

"Contracted," he said, "it's UNITAID."

It was a great idea. Of course, to change the name, I had to get the approval of Chirac and his advisers. At first they said it sounded too English, but, after two hours of discussion, they accepted it.

New name in hand, we continued our mission to sign up other countries. Chile agreed in March, and then it was time to seal the deal with the Norwegians. We thought we would get a good reception there, because the Norwegians were already giving 1 percent of their gross domestic product — one of the highest percentages in the world — in the form of official aid. In addition, the government of Norway was responsible for leading the effort to meet the fourth and fifth Millennium Development Goals, on child mortality and mothers' health.

Norway was important for us, too, because of the country's status in the WHO. Gro Harlem Brundtland, its former prime minister and also a doctor, had been head of the WHO until 2003. In 2006, Jonas Gahr Støre, who had been her cabinet director there and had become Norway's foreign minister, had created a group for foreign ministers to discuss the world's health crises — an essential initiative because it showed that problems of international health were major political problems as well. If Norway agreed to participate in UNITAID, other countries would surely follow.

Dussourd spoke to Sigrun Mogedal, who was then Norway's ambassador for HIV/AIDS in Geneva, where UNAIDS is based. She is a woman who would give her life for others, I think; for many years, at important moments on the international political stage, she has selflessly defended the health of mothers and children in poor countries. She thought UNITAID was an excellent idea, and she managed to get one of the prime minister's advisers involved as well. Within weeks, Norway agreed to be a founding member of UNITAID, with a tax on carbon emissions—not airline tickets—providing the revenue. The United Kingdom joined shortly afterwards, also with a different way of contributing, through direct funding from the central government. By the time we met any of the heads of state, all the work was already done. If it hadn't been, we wouldn't have met with them — that's the key to diplomacy.

IN THAT SAME MONTH of April 2006, I went to see Sepp Blatter at his office in Geneva. I told him all the tragic statistics about AIDS, tuberculosis, and malaria, diseases that were affecting many of the countries where soccer was growing by leaps and bounds.

"Yes, it's terrible," he said, "but why are you telling me?"

"Because you can change this, just you . . . if you can put our logo on the footballs of the World Cup."

"No one has ever done that, and I am afraid that Adidas has already made the balls."

It was true, the balls had already been manufactured — the tournament was starting just two months later in June. But Blatter came back with an idea for an exchange of balls with UNITAID stickers on them between the captains of the national teams before every match of the World Cup. This was something, at least, and it turned out to be what we needed. We would have our coming-out party, our introduction to the whole world, on the biggest stage in global sports.

Just before the World Cup, I had a press conference in Paris with Eric Solheim, Norway's minister of international development. The idea was to introduce the French to UNITAID, the organization they would soon be funding. At the end of the press conference, we asked the Cameroonian football star Samuel Eto'o and some other players to present the UNITAID balls. After that, it was official: Our name was in the public eye. Even though we were still just a few people working at the foreign ministry on the Quai d'Orsay in Paris, no one could deny what we were doing.

After the tournament, on July 30, we passed the law for the airline tax in France. The airlines would begin collecting the money in September. There was one final outcry in the press: Tour operators, travel agencies, and airlines all claimed that the tax would cripple their business. Of course, they still refused to look at the specifics of the tax and how it would work, and their protests were no more logical at that time than they had been initially. Implementing the tax in France wouldn't affect anyone who was thinking about a visit from abroad. Still, we had a public relations problem. Until our program could show some results — that is, all the great things that we would do with the money generated by the tax — it was hard for us to make our best case.

Jean-François Rial came to our rescue. He saw the stir in the press and was outraged. He knew that the logic behind the complaints was wrong, and he wrote an opinion article in *Le Monde,* the daily newspaper of the French establishment, explaining the fallacy. Rial wasn't a government official, an academic, or an expert on infectious diseases; he was the president of Voyageurs du Monde, one of France's largest tour operators. If a titan of the travel industry was supporting us, I knew we would eventually win the public relations battle. But more importantly, I saw that Rial understood our plan and cared about UNITAID.

Rial would become a vital part of UNITAID, even though his politics and mine were somewhat different. But on this issue we agreed, and I started including him in our weekly meeting on UNITAID's future. I even invited him along as I tried to persuade more heads of government to participate. Soon we became inseparable. While I looked the part of the senior politician in a dark suit and wire-rimmed glasses, he wore tiny horn-rims, an open-collared shirt, and loafers without socks. But we were both committed to the success of UNITAID, and it was Rial's genius that later helped us to make the greatest leap forward in UNITAID's history.

WITH RIAL'S INVOLVEMENT, the public relations problem in France — which, if people had simply stuck to the facts, should never have been a problem at all — was solved. Yet it wasn't long before I saw a real problem behind the scenes. Because this was a tax law, it was sponsored by the finance minister in the parliament, and officials from the finance ministry were put in charge of writing the regulations that would make the law a reality.

But when I saw the regulations they had written, I couldn't believe it: The money from the airline tax was going to go straight to the finance ministry, and each year the ministry would negotiate how much money UNITAID would receive. The finance minister was not personally responsible for this turn of events — he was on our side — but his administration had made an attempt to control the money. I called Chirac right away, and he was blunt in his instruction to the finance ministry; "I think there's a mistake in your regulation," he said. "I don't want any negotiations. I want the money to go to UNITAID."

The civil servants from the foreign ministry whom I had designated to work on UNITAID weren't always happy about their work, either. They complained that UNITAID was a health issue, not diplomacy, and diplomacy was what the foreign ministry was supposed to do. Their responsibilities did often involve working with foreign governments, but we also had to handle all the administrative tasks. We didn't have any personnel from the World Health Organization or anyone else; the French state provided all the manpower.

Nonetheless, we continued trying to sign up more countries. In the fall, I saw South Korea's foreign minister, Ban Ki-Moon, who would later become secretary-general of the United Nations. I told him that I thought it would be important for a country in Asia to join UNITAID — so far we were only in Europe, Africa, and Latin America — and he agreed.

Every three months during this process, I received a memo from Dussourd and Duneton, and every three months, I presented the memo to Chirac in an envelope at his Wednesday meetings of the council of ministers. When he opened the envelope, it was always good news about UNITAID. You could see that he was personally committed to the project, because he always said, "Yes, thumbs-up!" All the other ministers looked on enviously. Chirac was nearing the end of his political career, and the idea that France could lead a significant, international, humanitarian effort had become increasingly important to him. In fact, whenever we met with another head of state from that time onward, Chirac's first remark was always, "Mr. President, I want your country to join UNITAID." And then he would invite me to explain why.

The official launch of UNITAID, with all the attendant pomp and circumstance, took place during the UN's annual meeting in New York, in September 2006. Many foreign ministers were there, as well as the international media.

At last, it was time for UNITAID to spread its wings and leave the nest. We opted to create a base for the organization in Geneva, at the WHO, because we thought it would add credibility and also accountability to the organization. I asked Dussourd to be the executive secretary in charge of UNITAID's administration, but typically for him, he declined. "No, no, it's finished!" he said, and he was off to find another challenge. Instead, we chose Jorge Bermudez, a Brazilian expert on public health and vaccines who had served in various capacities in the WHO, and we made Duneton his number two. We also chose Elizabeth Hoff of Norway, an experienced staffer from the WHO, to lead our day-to-day operations; ever since, I have appreciated her intellectual rigor and her 100 percent engagement at every stage of UNITAID's development. We set up a board of which I was chairman, and we offered seats to the governments of our founding members: France, the United Kingdom, Norway, Brazil, and Chile. We added seats for Asia (represented by South Korea), the African Union, the WHO, the Bill & Melinda Gates Foundation (which had agreed to donate ten million dollars annually to UNITAID, our only private donation), patients' advocacy groups, and a consortium of nongovernmental organizations.

That last seat was held by Khalil Elouardighi, a French-Moroccan in his twenties who represented ACT UP (AIDS Coalition to Unleash Power), which had begun as an organization of gay men with HIV/AIDS and had transformed itself into an international organization dedicated to fighting the global epidemic.

Without Elouardighi, I could not have made UNITAID a success. He brought credibility to UNITAID and helped us to avoid opposition from nongovernmental organizations, even though we were new visitors on what was usually their turf. Dealing with them was new to me, and he always gave me his guidance. At each step, he took me aside and said, "Philippe, don't go there, but do go there." Sometimes it took two hours of discussion, but, in general, I was persuaded.

Like Bill Clinton, Elouardighi was convinced that UNITAID had to be innovative in its spending as well as its fund-raising. I was worried about the push-back from the foreign ministry, and so I wanted to give UNITAID a fast start, to show everyone some results. But Elouardighi said to me,

"We're on the right track, but we have to organize the strategy of UNITAID. And what is your strategy?"

"Oh, we're going to give these programs money . . ."

Immediately he stopped me. Like Clinton, he had a bigger ambition in mind and it was a crucial strategic vision: "No, we set up UNITAID to have a market impact on drugs, medicines, and the healthcare system. As a board member, I am going to refuse all the programs without market impact."

In some board meetings, Elouardighi annoyed people. He asked a lot of questions, and he didn't compromise easily. But most of the time, people followed him. They respected him. He was rarely wrong.

During those first months of 2007, I met another young person who would also become crucial to UNITAID's success. Laurence Thurion was a blogger I had encountered while promoting a book I'd written about French foreign policy. She disarmed me with her frankness from the start. "I didn't really want to come here, because I thought you were a politician like all the others," she said. "Now that I've met you, I don't understand why you're not the same on television as you were at lunch." Four months later, after I had left the government, she made an appointment with me. This time, she said, "I didn't see you in any newspaper, any communication, any photo, and I would like to know what you are doing." So I told her all about UNITAID, and she said she thought it was wonderful. I thought I could use a person like her, so I hired her. Now she is my right-hand woman.

BY APRIL 2007, we had twenty-three countries on board. Their leaders had all agreed to introduce the airline ticket tax, and at least half a dozen of them would be collecting it by the end of the year. It was time to go back to our harshest critic, the United States.

The United States had rejected the tax when we launched the program. I respected their decision, but I still decided to arrange a high-level meeting in Washington that month. Just as before, the members of the Bush administration were blunt. "It's a great idea," they said, "but do you know what your French historian Alexis de Tocqueville wrote about our country? It's all about freedom of choice. You say a child dies every thirty seconds from malaria. If I want to save him, fine, I can pay. But if not, I'm not going to pay."

It felt as though the sky had fallen on my head. The culture was so different. Obviously, the United States would never accept the airline ticket tax, and that refusal would make expanding UNITAID much more difficult; other countries would be able to point to the American logic to justify their own decisions not to participate. At the Monday morning meeting in Paris, I told the UNITAID staff and advisors what had happened. As I was bemoaning the situation, Rial interrupted me. The message from the United States was clear, he said: You have to let the traveler make the decision about whether to contribute or not. And that was not all. There was a surprisingly easy way to put the decision in the traveler's hands. Just three companies were responsible for two-thirds of the world's airline reservations. If you could work with those three companies, you could give hundreds of millions of travelers the option to make a contribution at the very moment that they bought their airline tickets.

This was news to me, and at first I couldn't believe what I was hearing. So I asked him whether the airline ticket reservation industry was really so centralized. If Rial was right, we wouldn't have to go government-to-government anymore, hat in hand. We could go straight to the industry and, with the agreement of just a few key executives, open the door to hundreds of millions of dollars of potential contributions.

The board of UNITAID met several times to discuss the idea of the voluntary contribution. A few members, from both governments and nongovernmental organizations, said we should commission a study from McKinsey & Company, the international consulting group, to validate our plan. It would give us credibility and add some numbers to what was so far just an idea. We asked the firm to estimate the cost of a study, and they came back with a budget of one million dollars. Rial hit the roof. He couldn't believe that so much money would be needed to analyze such a simple idea, especially an idea that he knew, given his experience in the travel industry, could work.

I knew I couldn't give up on the study, though. The board members were right; we needed some sort of document to show to our donors. It's easier to get a signature from Norway, the United Kingdom, the Gates Foundation, and the WHO when it's not just the foreign minister of France saying that the program will work. We needed some kind of authoritative, independent confirmation, even if it confirmed what we already knew. That was just the way things worked. So Duneton used his connections, and the official at the French embassy in Washington who was in charge of international aid called up the Gates Foundation. They thought we had a great idea and agreed to pay for the study; we were greatly indebted to the foundation, especially to Tachi Yamada and Joe Cerrell, who believed in UNITAID from the beginning. Rial agreed to be the main intermediary between UNITAID and McKinsey, and for four months they deluged him with materials: rafts of e-mails and hundreds of pages of research papers. At the end, of course, the study found that the voluntary contribution was a great idea.

So we went to work. By a happy coincidence, one of the senior executives of the three airline reservation companies, Philippe Chérèque of Amadeus, was an old friend of Rial from southern France. He assigned one of his colleagues, a corporate strategist named Kristel Lataste, to help us figure out how to make the voluntary contribution a reality. After we had figured out a way to incorporate the idea into Amadeus's reservation software, we could offer it to Travelport and Sabre, the other two giants in the industry. Together, the three companies accounted for roughly two billion airline ticket reservations every year.

The voluntary contribution began as a simple idea, but, as usual, even simple ideas can be difficult to implement. The more I immersed myself in the details, the more I realized the technical complexity of our project: We had started by obtaining the agreement of the leaders of just three companies, and somehow we were going to contact hundreds of millions of people through them.

As I was considering how to structure our approach, I had a fortuitous meeting with my successor as foreign minister, Bernard Kouchner. I told him what I was working on, and he said, "It's a great idea! Go for it!" I looked him right in the eyes and said, "The staff of UNITAID is working at 120 percent, and I can't keep asking them to put in overtime." Then he recommended a friend of his, Bernard Salomé, whom he had met when he was an administrator in Kosovo during the conflict there. "Bernard is the man you need, but at the moment he's advisor to the director of the Library of Alexandria project. I don't know if he'd accept the job." He gave me Salomé's telephone number, and the next day, I called him. A meeting was set. As I spoke to Salomé more and more, I could tell that he would say yes — mainly for reasons of generosity, ingrained since childhood by an uncle who had given his life to helping the less fortunate, and by two decades of work at the World Bank. He became the director of the project. The pitfalls were large and numerous, and he had plenty of occasions to rue the day that I involved him in this adventure. But like Dussourd, Duneton, and Hoff, he loved building things from the ground up, opening new pathways, and coming up with new ideas.

THE AGREEMENT WITH Chérèque proved to be the key element going forward. Thanks to him, we received contacts at
Sabre and Travelport. Whenever we ran into trouble in our
negotiations, we called him and he cleared the way for us.
Gordon Wilson, the chief executive of Travelport, quickly
agreed to participate, and I was impressed by how involved his
team became. It was tougher for us to get in touch with Sam
Gilliland and Tom Klein, the chairman and president, respectively, of Sabre, but once we did, they embraced the program
enthusiastically. I was struck by the motivation and engagement of these captains of industry in a social cause; it became
an example to me of what was possible.

One of the interesting things about these three companies
was that they were integrated into several facets of the travel
business: not just airline ticket reservations, but also hotels
and rental cars. With that in mind, we began pursuing the big
players in the other parts of the industry — always, as Rial
had first suggested, in areas where a few deals could capture a
huge share of the market. For example, Gilles Pelisson, the
chief executive of Accor Hotels (which owns the Sofitel,
Novotel, Mercure, Ibis, and Motel 6 chains, among others, for
a total of more than four thousand hotels worldwide), became
the first leader of his industry to agree that every one of his
customers would be given the chance to make a voluntary
contribution at check-out time.

In the meantime, with just the airline ticket tax and the
other contributions we received, UNITAID achieved stunning
results. The small staff worked first at the Quai d'Orsay and

then in our own offices. After I left the foreign ministry in the spring of 2007, I began to work full-time at UNITAID. It was amazing. In just three years, we raised $1.4 billion — at first, with only four or five civil servants working full-time and later with only a couple dozen people in our secretariat.

The effect of our fund-raising was immediate. We placed a huge order for antiretroviral drugs and paid for research that would convert the treatment regimen from over a dozen bottles of syrup per month into a few pills, lowering the price per dose and making it easier to take the medicine. We began paying to treat one hundred thousand children who had HIV/AIDS in 2007, and we added another one hundred thousand children in 2008; now we pay for the treatment of three out of four of all children receiving antiretroviral treatment in the developing world — and we have committed to treating them for the rest of their lives. We supported the development of child-friendly doses for tuberculosis drugs and helped all patients to get results of diagnoses more quickly. We bought twenty million bednets to combat malaria, almost a quarter of the world market. (There is not yet an effective vaccine for malaria, which has many varieties, so prevention is the short-term objective.) For all these drugs, we lowered the prices substantially, as much as 50 or 60 percent.

Since that first meeting with Bill Clinton, I have never changed course. It's like plowing a furrow — always follow a straight line. The work was compelling exactly because it was so difficult. But I knew, we all knew, that the work we were doing would make a real difference. Nothing is more inspiring.

Chapter 3

Innovative Financing and Innovative Spending

All labor that uplifts humanity has dignity and importance and should be undertaken with painstaking excellence.

— MARTIN LUTHER KING JR.

THANKS TO THE AIRLINE ticket tax and the voluntary contribution, UNITAID is poised to become one of the world's biggest donors to humanitarian causes. Hundreds of thousands of travelers have contributed to UNITAID, and this chapter explains how UNITAID has gathered and spent their money.

Since the beginning, UNITAID's strategy has been to commit its money where a big investment could be a game-changer: transforming how treatments are delivered, making previously out-of-reach treatments accessible to more patients, and lowering prices for medicines and other disease-fighting products by achieving a dominant position in the market. A prime example is the Affordable Medicines Facility—malaria (AMFm), a new program of the Global Fund to Fight

AIDS, Tuberculosis and Malaria that will pay bulk subsidies directly to the producers of the most effective antimalarial drugs so that they are priced affordably for poor consumers, even in the tiniest shops in rural areas.

With UNITAID's funding, the results of the program have been stunning by any measure. In partnership with the Global Fund, UNITAID will help to give patients almost thirty million of the most effective treatments, known as artemisinin-based combination therapy (ACT). A comprehensive treatment using the drugs used to cost patients six to ten dollars; the subsidy will bring the price down to just twenty to fifty cents to end the sickness and allow patients to return to productive lives.

Naturally, UNITAID and its partners on the ground are concerned about whether the drug retailers will actually pass on to their customers the savings created by the subsidies. Many of the retailers have never sold ACT treatments before because their customers couldn't afford them; in other words, the local market simply wouldn't bear a higher price. To head off potential problems, though, the AMFm will package the ACT treatments with distinctive branding and even, sometimes, with a suggested local price printed on the label. This measure will also help to prevent fake drugs from being sold.

As the program is implemented this year, UNITAID will help to finance roughly one-quarter of the ACT treatments needed worldwide every year. In addition, UNITAID has already purchased twenty million long-lasting, insecticide-treated bednets — roughly a quarter of the market in 2009

— to protect people against the mosquitoes that carry the malaria parasite. This enormous purchase will help to ramp up the capacity of the factories in developing countries that produce the bednets, eventually leading to greater availability and lower prices.

These efforts are part of a program led by the United Nations secretary-general's Special Envoy for Malaria, Ray Chambers. After a successful and internationally recognized career as a private equity investor, he decided to give the rest of his life to helping the less fortunate. The participation of people like him in the fight against epidemics is essential, because they bring private-sector effectiveness to a public-sector working culture. And they also understand better than anyone else how market-based tools can be used to improve social welfare.

UNITAID decided to follow this approach — harnessing the power of markets to raise large sums of money in short periods of time, alongside the other innovative financing mechanisms — for good reason. In the fight against epidemics, a big push is usually more successful than years of marginal effort, because it can meaningfully disrupt the spread of the disease by reducing both the number of contagious people and the prevalence of pathogens. Spending one million dollars a year in a small country with a big tuberculosis problem might stop the incidence of the disease from rising, but spending twenty million dollars in one year might actually help it to fall.

Large investments also open up new possibilities for bargaining with pharmaceutical companies and producers of preventive measures against disease. The prospect of tens or even hundreds of millions of dollars in guaranteed orders is often enough to convince the drug manufacturers to make the format, dosing, and packaging of their drugs more user-friendly, as well as to lower their prices.

This was the case in the treatment of children with HIV/AIDS. In the past, the necessary combination of drugs was available to children in poor countries only as a collection of syrups, as many as sixteen bottles per month containing different drugs. Parents had to dose out each of the syrups carefully, and taking the medicine was extremely difficult — even dangerous — if clean water was not available every day, because the drugs had to be washed down with water to curtail side effects. Many poor families living in rural areas have to walk miles to obtain clean water, so just treating a sick child might require many hours of labor — hours lost to productive employment or to parenting. And if any one of the syrups were unavailable, the treatment would be incomplete and potentially ineffective. Clearly, the patient's ability to follow the regimen of drugs — what doctors call compliance — was at risk in hundreds of thousands of cases.

To solve this problem, UNITAID and its partner, the Clinton HIV/AIDS Initiative (CHAI), approached makers of generic antiretroviral drugs in India with a proposal: If the companies would develop an easier way to treat children, UNITAID would guarantee hundreds of millions of dollars worth of orders, and CHAI would deliver the treatments on the ground. With so much money on the table, the response was immediate, and UNITAID paid a group of experts chosen by the World Health Organization to select the best treatments. The Indian pharmaceutical companies now produce three pills that children need to take only once a day. Less water is necessary to take the pills, there is no need to measure out doses, and the drugs are available at no cost to the families of the sick children.

Since the project began in 2007, more than 250,000 children have been added to the treatment rolls, at a cost of $146 million so far. Prices for pediatric antiretroviral drugs have been reduced by 60 percent. After just three years of purchasing medicines, UNITAID now finances the antiretrovirals received by three out of four children being treated for HIV/ AIDS in the developing world.

In addition to treating children who already have HIV/ AIDS, UNITAID has tried to stop new cases from arising by cutting the rate of mother-to-child transmission of the virus. Pregnant women with HIV can dramatically reduce the likelihood that their babies will carry the virus by following a preventive antiretroviral regimen. In its first two years, UNICEF and UNITAID's program monitored and treated over 100,000 pregnant women with HIV to stop their children from contracting the virus. It used a proven treatment regimen that, when followed carefully, is almost always successful. In 2009, the program expanded, and UNICEF tested almost 4 million pregnant women for HIV and began treating 143,000 more with antiretroviral drugs.

Progress against tuberculosis has also been startling. In less than three years, UNITAID has already paid to treat more than 565,000 children with tuberculosis by financing the Global Drug Facility of the Global Partnership to Stop Tuberculosis, led by the World Health Organization. UNITAID's investments, which will total $113 million between 2006 and 2011 on tuberculosis alone, have led to new drugs being introduced in the developing world and have also lowered the price of treatments substantially.

These success stories didn't happen by accident. Each program funded by UNITAID is the product of a careful selection process overseen by a panel of medical and scientific experts, organized in cooperation with the WHO. They review the applicants for UNITAID money on the merits, and then UNITAID's board has the final vote.

One special aspect of this process is that UNITAID always tries to fund programs in their entirety, rather than chipping in, say, 10 percent here and 15 percent there. That choice means that lifesaving programs — and patients — can count on UNITAID's support from start to finish, for as many years as the program can be effective. It also means that UNITAID has to manage its money carefully. Even though it collected $1.4 billion in its first three years of fund-raising, it spent only one billion. The rest of the money was saved in WHO accounts to guarantee that, for example, the two hundred thousand children who were receiving treatment against HIV/AIDS for the first time would continue to get the drugs they needed for years to come. That said, in the long term, UNITAID hopes to pass the baton for the treatment of these patients to non-innovative groups such as the Global Fund to Fight AIDS, Tuberculosis and Malaria, so that it can focus its resources on more game-changing investments. The Global Fund is a much bigger organization, with $18.7 billion in resources committed to fighting epidemics at the time of this writing, and it may be able to achieve even greater economies of scale in treatments.

UNITAID's own revenues have proven to be relatively dependable, even predictable. During the recent global economic crisis, donations to private charities dropped steeply across wealthy countries: American foundations saw their asset bases shrink, Canadian community groups started tapping their reserves in addition to annual donations, and the British charity Oxfam threatened to cut jobs. Yet the volume of air travel in UNITAID countries dipped by only about 5 percent. Because UNITAID already operates with such a broad margin between revenue and spending, there was no way that difference could affect its grant-making ability. Indeed, UNITAID still has lots of room to grow. Getting a large economy such as Japan to sign up with UNITAID would make a far greater positive difference to the bottom line than any negative effect that might have been felt as a result of the recession.

Even as UNITAID's revenue increases, its costs will stay very low. At the moment, its yearly operating budget is only about six million dollars, or less than 1 percent of its annual revenue. The more people who travel and opt to support UNITAID, the more its revenues will rise; its administrative framework, meanwhile, will stay the same.

BECAUSE OF UNITAID'S STATUS in the United Nations system as an arm of the World Health Organization, it cannot collect donations directly from private individuals. Instead, the voluntary contributions are collected by the Millennium Foundation — a not-for-profit group founded in November 2008 expressly for this purpose — and then channeled to UNITAID and the programs it funds. There are no handling fees; the entire contribution goes straight to the Millennium Foundation, which appears separately as the recipient of the funds on the donors' credit card statements.

To see how the voluntary contribution works, it's important to realize that an airline ticket can be purchased in several ways: through a retail travel agent, directly online, or through a business's corporate account. The three big bookers — Amadeus, Travelport, and Sabre — receive 80 percent of the reservations made by traditional travel agents. When the agents book airline tickets on their own computers, a pop-up window appears, prompting them to ask their customers if they would like to make a contribution. Thanks to the software developed with Amadeus, they won't have to enter the customers' credit card information twice; the contribution is added automatically to the final amount of the transaction. This is an important wrinkle that was discovered in the McKinsey study. In trials, customers who had to enter their credit card information twice were only one-quarter as likely to make the contribution.

Many online transactions work the same way, except without the travel agent as the middleman, because the big three bookers control some of the biggest websites, too. Opodo belongs to Amadeus; ebookers.com belongs to Orbitz, which is controlled by Travelport; and Sabre owns Travelocity and lastminute.com. Expedia is independent, but it, too, has signed on to the program. Together, these companies control the lion's share of reservations in the United States and Europe; the market truly is that concentrated. The Millennium Foundation is trying to sign an agreement with Priceline, the other market leader in the United States and Europe, as well as with individual airlines that sell tickets through their own websites and with other travel companies.

Contributions from tickets purchased by businesses will depend on agreements with corporate travel agents such as American Express, Carlson Wagonlit, and Thomas Cook. Businesses that want to participate will be able to institute a company-wide policy to make contributions with each reservation, or they will be able to leave the decision to individual travelers. In pursuing all these new agreements, the Millennium Foundation's strongest backer is Jean-Claude Baumgarten, the president and chief executive of the World Travel & Tourism Council, whose members are the leaders of the industry's top one hundred firms.

After the money comes into the Millennium Foundation, it is either stored in interest-bearing accounts or transferred to finance UNITAID's grants. Those grants will buy medicine to treat the three big infectious diseases, and they will also pay for preventive treatments: bednets to stop malaria and drugs to stop mother-to-child transmission of HIV. But you won't just have to take UNITAID's word for it. Soon, you will be able to see the results of your contribution on your computer screen.

With its corporate partners, UNITAID is developing software that will give you a tracking number each time you make a contribution. This number will be attached to a shipment of medicine or another disease-fighting product when it is prepared in the factory. You will then be able to enter a website where, using satellite tracking, you will be able to follow that shipment through every stage of its journey, from the factory to a village or town, often a continent away, and see how your contribution will help to save people's lives.

Not everyone will care to check what happens to a small donation of just a couple of dollars, but the idea of tracking the money is more than a gimmick. Human solidarity depends on empathy and understanding. To see where the money goes is to experience a real connection, however small the scale. Today, anyone can use a computer to look at a village with Google Earth or to read about a town on Wikipedia. Sometimes it takes a human connection to draw you to that place, however. Most of the contributors to UNITAID and the Millennium Foundation will be world travelers; perhaps, on some voyage in the future, they'll want to truly follow the money and travel to the places where their generosity made a difference.

This is the revolutionary potential of the program. To many people, official aid is just a collection of lines and numbers in their government's budget. The activities of international groups such as the World Bank, and even those of major charities, can be just as opaque because of the extensive bureaucracy, financial complexity, and political considerations involved in their decision-making processes. By contrast, UNITAID innovates not just by the way it raises and spends money, but also by creating direct and tangible connections between communities around the globe.

FOR ALL ITS UNIQUENESS, UNITAID does not operate in a vacuum. As we have already discussed, other innovative financing mechanisms are taking different approaches to the fight against epidemics. But there are certainly important opportunities to cooperate.

Take the example of the development of a new vaccine. Let's say that a researcher at a university in Switzerland has come up with a different way to fight tuberculosis, and she wants to start a small company to develop the vaccine. At the moment, she has a treatment that works in a test tube but must figure out a way to deliver it in humans. After that, she'll need to do human trials. There is broad consensus, however, that the treatment is promising and could lead to an effective vaccine.

To start the company and go through this process will cost about ten million dollars. This is where the innovative financing mechanisms can make a difference in the creation of treatments as well as their application. Perhaps one of the experts at the Global Alliance for Vaccines and Immunizations (GAVI), which directs the funds raised by IFFIm and the Advance Market Commitments for Vaccines (AMC), has heard about the Swiss researcher's work. He might then contact UNITAID to see if it would be willing to stump up the money to develop the vaccine. UNITAID might offer the money, but with the condition that the vaccine be offered at cost to developing countries if the human trials are successful. The expert could also talk to representatives of the AMC, which guarantees future prices for new drugs to ensure that they are developed. Having a fixed price would ensure that the researcher's company could cover her costs. Then he could approach the International Finance Facility for Immunization (IFFIm) to see whether its member countries would back a bond issue to pay for a large initial order of the vaccine. This order would provide a guaranteed market for the drug — something poor countries that might need the drug wouldn't be able to do on their own. And he might finish by consulting the Debt2Health initiative, in which wealthy countries forgive debts owed to them by poor countries if the poor countries promise to invest the freed-up money in medical treatments; through this mechanism, the poor countries themselves might be able to pick up part of the bill.

By working together, UNITAID, AMC, IFFIm, and Debt2Health would have given a small, uncertain venture the potential to transform itself into a sizeable producer of a blockbuster vaccine against tuberculosis. These things take time, of course, but the presence of the innovative financing mechanisms can greatly accelerate what might have been a slow and arduous process for the researcher, had she been acting on her own. She would have had to find investors who were willing to bet on a product with uncertain sales prospects, and then try to interest pharmaceutical companies in a drug whose main markets would be in poor countries, where prices might be too low to justify production and distribution.

Moreover, the innovative financing mechanisms' participation would have ensured that the vaccine would be available at a reasonable cost to the patients who needed it in the developing world. This is not a given in the pharmaceutical industry; often, companies have to focus on selling their drugs in wealthy countries, at higher prices, to make sure that their profits will be high enough to justify the costs of research and development. In the hypothetical example, had the researcher tried to develop the drug on her own, it's very likely that she would have been bought out by a large pharmaceutical company, which could have delayed the production of the vaccine and its arrival in the developing world. Most companies prefer to design the final product for sale in rich countries, recouping their research and development costs, before they consider distributing it in poor countries, at lower cost, and, as is sometimes necessary, in a different format.

Given these tendencies, it's not surprising that pharmaceutical companies devote enormous efforts to making non-lifesaving remedies for wealthy consumers, such as cures for baldness, heartburn, and erectile dysfunction, rather than creating drugs for epidemics that disproportionately affect poor people. This equation is changing, however, thanks to the innovative financing mechanisms. They can consolidate the demand from many different countries wracked by epidemics, so that pharmaceutical companies can more easily tap the potential market of the developing world. And the innovative financing mechanisms do this best when they work together.

Even in this collaborative group including UNITAID, AMC, IFFIm, and Debt2Health, UNITAID stands out as the only one of the four organizations that does not rely on governments to supply or guarantee the money that will be devoted to improvements in health. This is a meaningful distinction, because governments have a tendency to winner-pick or balance their commitments against each other.

There are clear political reasons for these phenomena. First, governments like to make positive headlines. Gordon Brown of the United Kingdom ushered IFFIm into the world, and his government is its biggest backer, with pledges of $130 million every year for a decade; it's his baby. Debt2Health received its first and largest commitment from Germany, which will have forgiven a total of $290 million in loans to the developing world between 2008 and 2010; Germany is the headline country for that initiative. If either of these governments had just given smaller amounts to a number of funds and financing mechanisms, they might not have captured the same glory for their leaders.

Additionally, governments like to get credit as many times as they can for the same thing. Let's say the United States pledges up to one hundred million dollars to guarantee a low price for next-generation antiretroviral treatments against HIV/AIDS in sub-Saharan Africa through the AMC. With this one pledge, politicians can generate several different headlines: "One hundred million dollars to fight AIDS," "One hundred million dollars in new aid for Africa," "One hundred million dollars for research into new drugs," and so on. The single pledge can be counted under several rubrics, too, thus contributing to goals set by previous legislation (for example, hypothetically, a goal to raise aid to Africa by ten billion dollars in five years). And the punch line, of course, is that the pledge is for a maximum of one hundred million dollars — in reality, less money might be needed to guarantee a low price for the treatments.

Together, these factors mean that governments aren't always the most reliable sources for aid, to say nothing of the problems they run into when their economies are in trouble, appetite for foreign aid declines, and their ability to raise money by issuing new bonds weakens.

UNITAID is not alone in going directly to product markets for aid money. (Product) Red works with major brands of clothing, electronics, and even credit cards to collect small donations through consumers' purchases. In Germany, part of the proceeds collected from selling carbon dioxide certificates — the "rights to pollute" that industrial companies trade among themselves under an overall cap on emissions — are being used to improve health in the developing world.

The use of different sources of funding helps to diversify the risks in the fight against disease. If one source dwindles or fails, others may be able to pick up the slack. But there are risks, too. One of the foremost is that people will look on these sources of funding as substitutes, rather than complementary tools, for a task that is too big for any of them to undertake alone.

Chapter 4

Innovative Financing and Society

Since you get more joy out of giving joy to others,
you should put a good deal of thought into the
happiness that you are able to give.
—— ELEANOR ROOSEVELT

THE STORY OF UNITAID is remarkable if only for the fact that so much was accomplished by so few people in so short a period of time. To succeed, UNITAID had to take advantage of its momentum and push forward, signing up new countries and funding new projects, as quickly as it could. But now that UNITAID is entering a new stage of its life with the launch of the voluntary contributions, let's step back for a moment and consider the bigger picture. Is there anything that UNITAID can do better? Is there anything that innovative financing as a whole can do better?

So far, we have described the motivations that led to the creation of the innovative financing mechanisms, and we have also recounted the events that led to the founding of UNITAID and the challenges from which the voluntary contribution was born. Shifting into the present, we explained how UNITAID works, and how it might cooperate with other innovative financing mechanisms to maximize their effectiveness as a group. But we have not yet discussed the deeper economic and philosophical issues that surround the use of innovative financing as a tool for helping developing countries. The responses of policymakers and the public to those issues will shape the future of UNITAID and of innovative financing as a whole.

The first and most essential question is whether UNITAID and its sister organization, the Millennium Foundation (which collects the voluntary contributions, as described in the preceding chapter), have the right goal. From the beginning, they have targeted the eradication of the three big epidemics in the developing world — in parallel with the sixth Millennium Development Goal — by sharing the gains of globalization as their founders intended. To be precise, the sixth goal is to reverse the spread of HIV/AIDS by 2015, make treatment for HIV/AIDS available to everyone who needs it by 2010, and reverse the spread of malaria and tuberculosis by 2015. With the approval of its board, UNITAID hopes to take on the goals for child and maternal health as well.

Together, these goals clearly compose a noble mission. But public health is only one ingredient of human and economic development. Given that a mechanism such as the tiny tax on airline tickets can raise huge sums in very little time and with little administrative cost, one has to ask: Is public health the best target for that money? Is it the most pressing need?

UNITAID justified making the fight against the epidemics its primary focus not merely on humanitarian grounds — after all, most people would agree without hesitation that helping the sick to recover is a good thing — but also by using the same kind of logic that a business owner would employ if faced with a choice of investing in several different projects. The owner would probably look for projects with high expected returns and relatively little uncertainty attached. In the fight against poverty, considerable uncertainty exists about the roles of things such as infrastructure, trade, access to credit, and legal institutions. All of them are important, but it's not always clear that you can improve them by spending aid money. Much less uncertainty exists about public health; in the most recent empirical studies, health is emerging as not just as an ingredient but as a prerequisite for economic growth in poor countries. Just as importantly, investments in health often have well-defined prices and well-defined results; we know how much it costs to buy drugs and deliver them, and we know that, if the drugs are taken correctly, they can save lives.

To be sure, the big three infectious diseases are not the only major killers in the world. In low-income countries, lower respiratory tract diseases such as pneumonia and acute bronchitis end more lives every year than HIV/AIDS, and three times as many as tuberculosis or malaria. Diarrheal diseases also rank higher on the mortality list. But lower respiratory tract diseases and diarrheal diseases are blanket categories that embrace a variety of ailments caused by viruses, bacteria, pollution, and even fungi. Attacking them requires not just drugs for treatment but improvements in infrastructure and changes in cultural norms: building pumping stations and purification plants for clean water, constructing sanitary latrines in cities and rural villages, and educating the public about washing hands and food.

Groups such as the World Bank and the United Nations Development Program have been working on these other issues for many years, and they are arguably just as urgent as the fight against the big three infectious diseases. UNITAID and the Millennium Foundation chose a different focus, however, because of the economic dynamics of lifesaving drugs. It is much easier to influence the market — increasing supply and lowering prices — in the case of medical treatments than in the case of latrines. Latrines are generally constructed on site, with labor and construction materials purchased locally; it would be difficult, though not impossible, to mass-produce latrines and then ship them to poor neighborhoods around the world. Even in that case, the latrines would have to be installed locally, with all the attendant plumbing, at extra cost. There is no doubt that sanitation efforts could benefit from innovative financing, but for now, innovative spending might be hard to achieve.

In short, UNITAID and the Millennium Foundation chose to fight the big three epidemics because that is where the bang for the buck of their innovative financing and innovative spending seemed to be the greatest. When that ceases to be the case — perhaps, if we are so lucky, when the tide is turned against all three epidemics — the powerful lever of innovative financing could well be applied somewhere else. Indeed, UNITAID will continue to exist after 2015, when the deadlines for the Millennium Development Goals elapse. It is committed to treating its HIV/AIDS patients for the rest of their lives, until another group such as the Global Fund can take over their treatment, or until a complete cure for the virus is discovered. And it will continue to seek to influence markets for treatments that can stop epidemic diseases, even if other diseases replace the big three as the best targets.

The second question about UNITAID is whether it is set up to maximize its effect on its chosen goal. It began as a small team in the French foreign ministry, and then became an agency attached to the World Health Organization. There were three significant reasons for this change. First and foremost, as the organization grew and became more international, it was no longer appropriate for it to reside within the foreign ministry; it needed a board that represented the interests of all its stakeholders, both from donor and recipient countries. Second, being housed at the WHO, with that august organization's official imprimatur, gave UNITAID credibility and trustworthiness, which were of utmost importance given the gigantic sums of money that it would be handling and its continual lobbying to involve more countries in its efforts. And third, as part of the WHO, UNITAID would have access to an expansive network of political connections and scientific expertise that would be critical to its success.

These factors allowed UNITAID to achieve so much, with so little staff, in so little time. For that, UNITAID must acknowledge the help of Lee Jong-wook and Margaret Chan, the two directors-general of the WHO who made innovating financing for health a priority. But being housed at the WHO, which is part of the United Nations, brought limitations as well. It made UNITAID part of a much-maligned bureaucracy that was significantly less agile and dynamic than an organization in the private sector would be.

So there is potentially a tradeoff: greater networking and credibility versus less responsiveness to new developments. This tradeoff, however, may eventually disappear if UNITAID manages to achieve it goals. At that point, the Millennium Foundation — which, as an independent not-for-profit organization, could continue to collect voluntary contributions — would be able to build on UNITAID's success as it devoted itself to other worthy causes.

WITHIN THIS CONTEXT of opportunities and limitations, UNITAID operates largely as we described in the preceding chapter. Its practices evolved in a short time, however, and that evolution was driven at times by political considerations. Now that UNITAID has reached a level of maturity in fundraising and in dispensing its money, we can ask: Does UNITAID do these things as well as it possibly could?

Starting this year, the two main components of UNITAID's fund-raising will be the airline ticket tax and the voluntary contribution. Together, they will raise hundreds of millions of dollars annually to finance the fight against HIV/AIDS, malaria, and tuberculosis. These activities are not neutral for the global economy; they affect the donors, the recipients, and also other participants in the markets where the money is collected and spent.

To start, let's consider the tax. Economists tend to favor taxes with broad bases and low rates because, as a rule, they do not discourage much economic activity. For instance, a two-dollar-per-ticket tax on a market of two billion airline tickets will generate a much milder response from consumers than a two-hundred-dollar tax on a market of twenty million tickets. Consumers in the second market, which might be equivalent to the air travelers in one small but wealthy country, would probably buy many fewer tickets if they faced such a heavy levy. By contrast, the effect of the two-dollar tax on ticket sales in the larger market is likely to be almost negligible. In fact, many air travelers may not even perceive the tax at first, because so many larger taxes and fees are added to tickets at the time of purchase.

The fact that the tax is on airline tickets matters, too. Air travel has effects on the economy that go beyond the effects on the people who fly, because airplanes generate huge amounts of pollution. A tax on a polluting product can actually improve the efficiency of the economy by discouraging people from doing something that has a social cost. Some taxes on air travel and airplane fuel can already be justified with this argument. So, if the two-dollar tax does indeed discourage a little bit of flying — and, to be clear, we think that it probably won't to any perceptible degree — that decrease might actually be efficient from the point of view of social welfare.

Finally, the two-dollar tax is special because it is a lump sum. It doesn't matter if you buy a discounted or full-fare ticket; the tax is the same. As a result, the tax doesn't enter into a big part of the typical decision faced by tourists and business travelers. The timing of your trip doesn't affect the tax, either, even though the prices of tickets may change from day to day. As taxes go, this one is about as benign as you can get.

Now, what about the voluntary contribution? According to the McKinsey study mentioned in previous chapters, it could become just as important a fund-raising mechanism as the tax during the next several years. And indeed, encouraging precedents exist for the concept of voluntary contributions tied to specific parts of the economy.

Many Americans will recall the March of Dimes, which began during Franklin Roosevelt's presidency as an independent fund-raising program to fund research in poliomyelitis, the disease that put Roosevelt in a wheelchair in his later years. After his death, Roosevelt's face was added to the dime, as a permanent encouragement to Americans to donate this small piece of change. As in the case of UNITAID, the March of Dimes realized that millions of small donations could add up to substantial sums.

The link between air travelers and donations to causes in the developing world is nothing new, either. UNICEF's

Change for Good campaign has seen flight attendants collecting travelers' loose or leftover coins and currency since 1987, accumulating more than seventy million dollars over its lifetime. The idea of adding a small donation to an unrelated transaction has been tried before, too. Customers on eBay's auction websites are routinely asked whether they want to donate one dollar to a randomly selected cause when they pay for items that they've won. Supermarket chains such as Argentina's Disco are also in on the act, with cashiers asking customers if they'd like to round up their purchase to the nearest peso by donating the difference to local charities.

Clearly, people are willing to consider combining donations to charitable causes with their everyday lives. But linking the world's wealthier consumers — the ones who buy most of the world's airline tickets — to poor people suffering from infectious diseases in countries thousands of miles away could be more of a stretch. One way that existing charities attempt to bridge that divide is by allowing donors to choose the people they help. Some charities work with people of specific ethnic or religious groups. Others send prospective donors photographs of the people whom they might help.

In this context, one unavoidable question is how much say the voluntary contributors should have in the use of their voluntary contribution. Before the voluntary contribution was launched, the chief executive of an Islamic bank based in Saudi Arabia offered a big donation to UNITAID, on the condition that it would be used to fund treatments in Islamic countries.

The gift was refused. But is it so unreasonable for an air traveler from Madagascar, one of the poorest countries that currently collects the airline ticket tax, to ask that her payment be used to help other people from Madagascar? UNITAID's rules don't permit this, and the Millennium Foundation doesn't plan to, either, with the money from voluntary contributions. As a result, some travelers might decide to donate to local charities rather than making a contribution to help citizens of other countries. This problem could be especially acute among travelers from poor countries, given that as much as 15 percent of UNITAID's money can actually be used for treatments in middle-income countries; they might not want to send money to a place where living standards are higher than those in their own communities.

In addition to these issues, economic considerations linked to the tiny tax and the voluntary contribution go beyond the decisions of individuals in specific markets and begin to enter the macroeconomic sphere. For example, because UNITAID and the Millennium Foundation will be financed almost exclusively by the airline tax and voluntary contributions, they face a special kind of risk. During an economic downturn, their revenues from both sources are likely to fall. We already know that purchases of airline tickets dropped about 5 percent during the recent crisis, and it's likely that individual donations would be even more sensitive to economic conditions. That's because the voluntary contribution is just that — voluntary; a person or a company whose budget is already being squeezed might be looking for any way, however small, of cutting costs.

At the same time, however, the need for money and treatments is likely to rise. Poor countries face a triple-whammy during an economic downturn: reductions in official aid as wealthier countries focus on protecting their own people, less money coming in as direct investment from the private sector, and lower prices for the commodities that are usually the poor countries' main exports. So, just as the need for help is cresting, the flow of money coming in is likely to hit a trough.

The way to deal with this problem is with long-term planning that creates a financial cushion in good times for use in bad times. UNITAID spends only a fraction of the money that it controls at any one time; there is a cushion in its coffers. However, its commitments to grant money to other organizations are usually set out over the long term; in fact, UNITAID is supposed to commit all its funds to grantees within a year of receiving them through the airline tax and the voluntary contribution. If those grantees need more money to deal with cyclical changes, will UNITAID be able to react? What is certain is that if UNITAID's innovative financing is diversified between revenues from the airline ticket tax and voluntary contributions, and if the sources for the contributions were spread around the world, UNITAID will be better protected than most donor organizations in the event of a recession or crash. Thus, the more UNITAID grows, the more effective UNITAID will be.

NOW THAT WE HAVE discussed UNITAID's goal, its organizational setup, and its financing practices, we can begin to debate how UNITAID should interact with the many other groups that are working toward the same and related goals. As we said in the preceding chapter, UNITAID does not operate in a vacuum. Other entities — government agencies, international bodies, private foundations, nongovernmental organizations, and other innovative financing mechanisms — are working toward the same Millennium Development goals. UNITAID has taken a leading role in financing the fight against the three big epidemics in a short period of time. But there is still the question of whether this constellation of entities, especially the innovative financing mechanisms, is currently organized for the greatest possible effectiveness. Are too many groups trying to raise money for the same causes? Can they possibly coordinate their activities? Or, on the contrary, are there too few organizations? The short answer is that coordination could be improved and having more organizations would probably help.

Economics offers several bits of theory and evidence to suggest that having multiple organizations trying to achieve the same goal can be useful. Consider the two innovative financing mechanisms that approach consumers directly: the Millennium Foundation (through the voluntary contribution) and Product (Red), which gives the Global Fund a share of the profits from Red-branded products ranging from Dell Computers and Microsoft software to Converse sneakers and American Express cards. Economists ask the question: If a person bought a Red-branded watch from Emporio Armani yesterday, would that affect their decision to contribute to the Millennium Foundation as they were buying an airline ticket today? It's possible that the person might say, "Well, I already made a donation yesterday, so I don't have to make one today." But even so, having both programs is not a bad idea. Some people will respond to Product (Red), some will respond to the voluntary contribution, and some will respond to both.

Empirical evidence suggests that people may indeed react positively when faced with many options for achieving the same goal; Americans planning for retirement, for example, tend to save more when they are given several ways to save. Another somewhat related theory takes the example of a saver — any saver — choosing which investments to put into a portfolio. The goal is to make money, and a fixed amount of savings is available to invest. A mathematical proof shows that the saver should put some amount of money into all possible investments that aren't clearly inferior to the rest of the options on the table. In other words, you wouldn't put any money into Investment A if it offered the same return but broader risks than Investment B, nor would you choose Investment A if it offered the same risks but a lower return than Investment C. But you *would* put money into every investment for which neither of those relationships held true.

Using that logic, you might expect a person who wants to help in the fight against disease to pursue his or her goal using all the possible options that weren't clearly inferior to each other. You might decide to give a total of five hundred dollars over the course of a year, but you'd split that up among various charities, innovative financing mechanisms, and official organizations. Of course, some people do just the opposite; they prefer to give a lump sum to one organization, perhaps because they think that a bigger gift will have a greater effect, or will show their loyalty to the organization, or will reflect better on them as donors, or might generate less junk mail. Having the other options available, however, doesn't make these people want to donate less money. The question is whether the amount is spread among several groups or given to just one; either way, it's still five hundred dollars.

Now, let's return to the earlier point about adding more options for achieving a given goal. Suppose that the hypothetical donor had not fixed the amount to give, but instead that the amount was affected by the number of options available. Will having more options raise the total amount, as the example of retirement saving suggested? Or, alternatively, could adding more options be detrimental to the donor's willingness to give? Might the donor be discouraged from giving altogether if the sheer number of outstretched hands seemed overwhelming or oppressive?

Put another way, UNITAID must ask whether there is a risk that, if voluntary contributions are collected on airline tickets, hotel bills, mobile phone payments, stock trades, and other transactions, consumers will simply grimace and say no to all of them. It's not hard to imagine an analogy from everyday life. Let's say you walk down the street every day and always see the same beggar. One week, perhaps because you're feeling magnanimous, you give the beggar a dollar four days in a row. Then, on the fifth day, three more beggars show up hoping to receive a dollar as well. Feeling mildly exploited, you shake your head and walk away.

Yet one idea from economic research actually says that the opposite may occur. An analysis of the breakfast cereal industry suggests that the dominant companies in the market bring out money-losing varieties of cereal to ensure that they control every possible point on the cereal spectrum. That way, other companies do not have any point of entry in the market; for example, a new company planning to introduce a chocolate-graham-cracker-flavored cereal with blueberry marshmallows would think twice if Kellogg's, the market leader, already offered one. In other words, Kellogg's keeps a firm grip on the consumer by making sure that its products fulfill every possible breakfast-cereal-related whim and that there is no excuse for the consumer to go elsewhere. So, if the international community offered every possible way of donating to the fight against HIV/AIDS, tuberculosis, and malaria, individuals and governments might not have any excuse *not* to donate to the cause.

Of course, this example doesn't account for the people who, bowled over (so to speak) by the plethora of cereal options, might decide to have eggs for breakfast instead. In the field of international aid, it would be like saying, "I'm fed up with all the grabbing hands for epidemics in the developing world. I'm going to donate to literacy projects instead." But then again, you wouldn't expect Kellogg's to adopt a strategy to preserve its market share if that same strategy was continually reducing the size of the market itself. In other words, there aren't many people switching to eggs.

Still, with so many organizations collecting money to meet the same goals — and all of them implicitly competing for the attention of politicians and consumers — one possible danger is that some people will become desensitized, if not completely disillusioned. "Why should I make a voluntary contribution," you might ask yourself, "if the AMC, the IFFIm, and the Global Fund are already receiving billions of dollars to fight these diseases?" This is a legitimate question. The problem is that even with all these groups raising money, the total amount they can devote to eradicating the big three infectious diseases is still far less than what is needed. Still, the danger of being desensitized — "donor fatigue," you might call it — behooves them to do everything they can to publicize the need for more funds.

Even publicity is perilous, however, and can generate its own kind of fatigue; there is no pleasure in hearing repeatedly about people dying by the hundreds of thousands in the developing world. For that reason, it is important for aid groups to emphasize a positive message: "Because of your donations, we saved two hundred thousand lives," or "Your gift gives back to you, with more consumers buying your country's exports and less instability in the regions where you might like to travel and do business."

Indeed, the psychological element is crucial in the pursuit of donations. If someone holding a sign on the street asks you for a two-dollar donation to fight disease, your response might not be the same as when you are sitting in front of your computer buying a one-thousand-dollar airline ticket. Context matters. For this reason, a bevy of organizations approaching people in several different ways might increase the total amount of money raised.

Having many organizations collecting money might also help donors feel pivotal — in other words, that their contribution would really make a difference. If only one entity was collecting money, you might feel as though your donation would be lost in a sea of bureaucracy or dwarfed by much bigger contributions from wealthy individuals and foundations. You might also want to be specific about where your donation went: to fight malaria, for example, but not HIV/AIDS or tuberculosis. Each of these arguments suggests that there might not be enough organizations collecting money.

Yet centralization of the aid effort — putting all fund-raising under one roof — also has obvious benefits. To understand why, consider an example from the academic sphere. In the mid-1990s, Harvard University asked its alumni for billions of dollars in donations as part of a massive campaign to enlarge its endowment. In many cases, the university allowed the alumni to decide how their money would be used: to hire new professors, maintain the dormitories, improve the sports programs, and so on. Year after year during the campaign, one essential part of the university came up short: the libraries. Harvard's officers were worried that without air conditioning and climate control in the university's libraries, thousands of books would disintegrate. But despite their pleas, the money didn't come in. Perhaps the alumni didn't have fond memories of their time spent in the stacks, or perhaps, as one dean suggested, air conditioning and climate control just weren't sexy enough. For whatever reason, the donations alone weren't enough to keep the libraries operating at a high standard; for the university to achieve its vision of a modern library system, it would have to use some of the funds that flowed from the very endowment that it was trying to enlarge.

The lesson was that if you allowed donors to choose where every dollar went, some objectives might be left unfulfilled simply because they weren't popular. Without a centralized organization distributing the funds raised by innovative financing, the same could happen in the fight against disease. For example, what if no one donated money to fight tuberculosis? Malaria patients might get the world's very best treatment, while hundreds of thousands of tuberculosis patients suffered for the lack of any medicine at all. You'd hardly be getting the best bang for your buck if you didn't even treat the easiest, most accessible tuberculosis patients.

This dynamic shows why it's important to diversify investments, too. Because UNITAID tries to bring down prices and improve treatments through its investments, it won't necessarily want to keep funding the same treatment program until it covers 100 percent, or even 50 percent, of the people who have a given disease. For example, it's possible that after half the people who need a treatment are already receiving it, production of that treatment will already be so efficient, and orders for it will already be so huge, that there will be no way to bring prices down further. In a case like this, it might be better for UNITAID to focus its next game-changing investment on bringing down the price of another drug, perhaps for a different disease, while the remaining sufferers of the first disease receive treatments paid for on a year-by-year basis through regular foreign aid and local budgets. There would be no need for another enormous guaranteed order worth tens of millions of dollars over several years.

According to this logic, only by spreading resources across different diseases and treatments can the innovative financing mechanisms get the best bang for their buck. That's not the only argument for coordination, of course. With many different groups raising money, there may also be a lot of duplicated effort: many publicity campaigns instead of one, many back-office operations, many research panels deciding which programs to fund, and so on. Eliminating these overlaps and redundancies could free up more money and time for the fight against disease. But bringing all the organizations under one roof could be difficult, because each one has different partnerships with governments and the private sector.

At the very least, the various groups could coordinate to improve their performance. Using that logic, Ban Ki-Moon, who brought South Korea into UNITAID and is now secretary-general of the United Nations, set up the H-8 group of the top international organizations for health: the WHO, the Global Fund, UNICEF, the Joint UN Program on HIV/AIDS, the Gates Foundation, GAVI, the World Bank, and the UN Population Fund. To take the coordination a step further, Philippe Douste-Blazy led the creation of the I-8 group of the innovative funding mechanisms that had its first meeting in May 2009. The members are UNITAID, the Millennium Foundation, IFFIm, AMC, (Product) Red, Debt2Health, the Responsible Social Investment Initiative of the French Development Agency, and a nascent program for collecting revenue from the market for carbon emissions trading.

As A GROUP, the innovative financing mechanisms have been welcomed wholeheartedly by some people in the field of development aid and more cautiously by others. The sheer size of the innovative financing mechanisms has elicited some worried reactions from nongovernmental organizations involved in the fight against the big three infectious diseases. For one thing, many smaller organizations cannot compete with the marketing campaigns undertaken by mechanisms that approach the consumer directly, such as (Product) Red. The smaller groups might fear that consumers who would ordinarily have sent them donations would choose to donate through innovative financing mechanisms instead.

Also, many nongovernmental organizations depend on official aid, in addition to private donations, for a large part of their funding. It may leave a bitter taste in their collective mouths to see heads of state celebrating the launch of the voluntary contribution, for example, even as these leaders and their colleagues freeze or trim official aid in the wake of the global economic downturn. Naturally, nongovernmental organizations might feel an acute threat that money previously distributed to them through official aid will be replaced by money collected from consumers and then distributed to a few big organizations by the Millennium Foundation and UNITAID.

This issue is of paramount importance for all innovative financing mechanisms. They were created to close the gap between official aid and the huge sums needed to turn the deadly tide of the three big epidemics once and for all. If governments start to use them as a substitute for official aid, the very purpose of their existence will be defeated. To avoid this eventuality, the Millennium Foundation and other independent or quasi-independent entities will have to hold governments to account, whether by shaming them publicly for cutting aid budgets or by holding them to promises to continue increasing aid at least enough to keep up with inflation.

The responsibility of the innovative financing mechanisms is therefore twofold: to accomplish their goals of fighting poverty and disease, and to ensure that their work does not go for naught. But trying not to replace official aid is only one part of fulfilling that responsibility. The other part is making sure that the programs in which the innovative financing mechanisms invest are genuinely effective. Programs seeking financing need to be assessed based on common criteria — for example, productive years of life saved per dollar invested — and existing programs need to be judged using high-quality data and rigorous statistics.

Development economics is making significant strides in this area, which is generally called impact evaluation, and all aid organizations, whether or not they use innovative financing, should take advantage. But for groups that raise money from private citizens, such as UNITAID and (Product) Red, impact evaluation is an absolute necessity. Unlike government agencies or international organizations, their very existence will come into question if donors doubt that their contributions are used effectively. If that happens, their funding will dry up rapidly.

People who make voluntary contributions will undoubtedly want to see results — and that is one of the great benefits of the voluntary contribution. This mechanism essentially enrolls the donor as an inspector of the program's effectiveness, ability to communicate its message, and willingness to share with donors its successes and ambitions. If, after five or ten years, progress against the epidemics seems slow, donors to these programs could well have a change of heart. Maintaining their engagement with the Millennium Development Goals will be a critical challenge in the future.

Chapter 5

The Future of UNITAID

Do your little bit of good where you are; it's those little bits of good put together that overwhelm the world.
— DESMOND TUTU

TOGETHER, UNITAID and the Millennium Foundation have joined the fight against the three big epidemics, alongside the governments and nongovernmental organizations that already commit billions of dollars and millions of hours of work to the cause every year. Despite this massive international effort, the problem is far from solved. The gap in funding is enormous — perhaps tens of billions of dollars per year — and viral resistance to known treatments is growing. The more the world waits, the harder it will be to turn the tide.

For that reason, UNITAID is setting ambitious challenges for itself, such as extending the airline ticket tax to new countries and expanding innovative financing into other industries. If the top fifty countries by purchases of airline tickets imposed the tax, UNITAID could raise several billion dollars a year, which might be enough to achieve the primary Millennium Development Goals for health in developing countries:

reverse the spread of HIV/AIDS by 2015, make treatment for HIV/AIDS available to everyone who needs it by 2010, and reverse the spread of malaria and tuberculosis by 2015.

UNITAID is also finding new ways to partner with pharmaceutical companies and on-the-ground aid groups to push for innovative spending. It is in the midst of creating a "patent pool" to simplify the transfer of intellectual property from the major developers of drugs against the big three infectious diseases to the manufacturers that can produce them en masse for the developing world. The goal is to speed the delivery of lifesaving medicines and to transform the way those medicines are taken so that treatment regimens are easier to follow. The idea is a powerful one for improving public health. Interestingly, the precedent came from quite a different field.

In the early 1990s, electronics companies around the world were trying to develop a new medium for recording, storing, and playing video. VHS tapes were clunky and took ages to rewind and fast-forward, just like the cassettes that had previously dominated the music industry. Two joint ventures, one between Toshiba of Japan and Warner of the United States, and the other between Philips of the Netherlands and Japan's Sony, were both working on formats that used discs similar to CDs that could be read by lasers. As the two joint ventures moved forward, other companies entered the mix, patenting technologies that would be useful for producing and reading the discs.

The problem was that both joint ventures were coming up with products that could, in theory, be viable for consumers. But a consumer who bought a machine to read Toshiba/

Warner discs wouldn't necessarily be able to use discs produced for a Philips/Sony machine, and vice versa. Just as VHS had eventually replaced Betamax as the standard for videotapes, one winner would probably emerge, meaning that the other joint venture had wasted its money. And as in the case of videotapes, both systems had their advantages. The Toshiba/Warner discs could store more data, but Philips/Sony had created a more robust system for reading and writing the data on the discs. In 1995, under pressure from computer and software firms, the electronics companies joined to create the DVD Consortium, through which they would share technology and launch the optical disc format that is ubiquitous in the world today. In the end, the companies combined the best aspects of both technologies in a single device; they shared their intellectual property, and they shared the proceeds.

The same kind of consortium would be needed to create what for many doctors and patients in the developing world is just a dream today: a single pill that can deliver effective treatment for one of the big three infectious diseases. UNITAID has already driven down the sixteen bottles of syrups needed each month to treat HIV/AIDS to a simple combination of three pills per day. But sometimes all three pills are not available — a local pharmacy might simply run out of one or two of them — so patients miss out on crucial parts of their therapy. Imagine how compliance with treatment regimens would improve if patients had to swallow just one pill.

The first step toward a patent pool is to organize a consortium between all the companies that make the ingredients for the three drugs in the usual treatment regimen. Then, with research funding and orders from UNITAID and other initiatives, they can try to develop the single-pill version of the treatment. UNITAID has already convinced the pharmaceutical companies Gilead (based in California), Johnson & Johnson's Tibotec (from Belgium), and Cipla (from India) to come together and offer a combination pill to fight HIV/AIDS. Now UNITAID is trying to do the same with companies that own patents for drugs to treat malaria and tuberculosis, as well as with producers of antiretrovirals.

The companies are understandably reticent in these matters; they don't want to share their patents, which are the products of hundreds of millions of dollars of research, and they also worry that a single-pill treatment created for poor countries would end up being smuggled into wealthy countries, destroying the markets where they make most of their profits. The World Trade Organization's arcane rules about the licensing of patented formulas for medicines, set down in a joint declaration by the group's members in 2003, complicate the issue further. Under these rules, some countries may legally allow companies to produce drugs without the permission of the owners of the drugs' patents, but their ability to export those drugs to countries that lack homegrown pharmaceutical industries is not always clear.

By contrast, UNITAID's approach is strictly voluntary; it tries to involve the pharmaceutical companies by appealing to their sense of solidarity rather than trying to force them to share their patents through laws or global trade rules. In exchange, UNITAID promises to deliver enormous demand for the new products that the companies might develop to fight the big three infectious diseases. It uses the carrot, not the stick.

Meanwhile, UNITAID is pursuing another opportunity for innovative spending: a quantum leap in the quality of treatment for HIV/AIDS patients in the developing world. At the moment, the vast majority of patients in poor countries receive first-generation antiretroviral treatments, which were developed in rich countries and prescribed as early as the 1980s. Second-generation antiretroviral treatments, however, are at least as successful in staving off the disease's worst symptoms, require fewer pills each day, and have fewer side effects, especially for patients who don't yet have full-blown AIDS. But to deliver these second-line drugs in the most effective way, doctors must track the level of viral activity in their patients' bloodstreams; patients with a higher "viral load" receive different drugs from those with lower levels of the virus in their blood. To do this requires technology, and technology is expensive.

In essence, to provide the best possible second-line therapy, you would go to villages in some of the poorest countries in the world — mostly in sub-Saharan Africa and Southeast Asia — and install the same kinds of machines used by hospitals in rich countries to measure a patient's viral load. But UNITAID hopes to create a new, cheaper technology that will accomplish this one test. It has already put out a call for proposals, not just to develop the equipment but also to distribute it across the developing world and train the people who will use it in far-flung locales. The program will be costly, but it could greatly improve the quality of life for hundreds of thousands of HIV/AIDS patients.

In cooperation with the Clinton HIV/AIDS Initiative, UNITAID has already cut the price of second-line antiretrovirals produced for developing countries in half, from \$315 annually to \$159, by negotiating large orders with the drugmakers. These treatments turn AIDS into a manageable chronic disease, rather than a terminal one, allowing celebrities such as the basketball star Earvin "Magic" Johnson to live for many years (eighteen at the time of this writing) after being diagnosed. Putting patients on second-line treatments also makes them less contagious, reducing the risk to other people.

These ambitious projects will help to improve access to medicine and preventive measures for poor people, but innovative spending demands that we also ask ourselves whether we can make investments with more fundamental, lasting effects. Can we improve the underlying framework for the purchase and delivery of treatments? Is it possible to reimagine the entire health systems of developing countries?

These are crucial questions because simply buying drugs is not enough to save lives. A recent visit to Ouagadougou, in Burkina Faso, revealed that shipments of antitretrovirals were arriving at the central dispensaries but the refrigerators in which they were stored had shut down for lack of electricity, potentially ruining the drugs. Because of problems like this, UNITAID approached the World Bank in 2008 with a ground-

breaking idea: to work with the governments of five developing countries to revolutionize their health systems, creating
not just flimsy imitations of a wealthy country's system, but
health systems truly adapted to their individual needs.

In a five-year experiment, this project will attempt to show
the massive economic gains that might be unlocked if a country underwent a public health transformation, with the big
three infectious diseases — and others — brought under control using innovative financing and innovative spending. So far,
this unprecedented project is just an idea, but it could make a
dramatic difference in the lives of millions of people. In the
past, economic research has indeed shown that improvements
in public health lead to stronger economic growth and higher
living standards. But no one has ever performed this kind of
experiment — an experiment on an entire country.

UNITAID's hope is that, should this experiment prove successful, no one will be able to deny the results; no poor country's government will be able to persuade its people that
spending money on guns will be better than spending money
on drugs, and no rich country's government will be able to
argue that sending aid is like pouring money down a well.
UNITAID's strategy will not be to duplicate, say, France's
public health system in Chad. Instead, it will try to tailor the
system to the countries' needs, demonstrating the flexibility
of its approach across a group of countries with different
health situations.

This last project will certainly provoke a series of arguments about the practicality, the effectiveness, and the

morality of taking over an entire country's health system — even (or especially) with the cooperation of that country's government. Yet to achieve its mission of innovative financing and innovative spending, the leadership of UNITAID believes that it must consistently challenge established ideas about the development, purchase, and delivery of medical treatments. This is what combining innovative financing and innovative spending means.

EVEN WITH THE SUDDEN and striking success of UNITAID and the other innovative financing mechanisms, there is still much work to do. For example, although it is true that UNITAID will help to deliver tens of millions of ACT treatments against malaria every year, that seemingly gigantic figure is tiny next to the 350 million to 500 million cases of malaria that arise annually. If governments will not raise their commitments of money and resources, innovative financing will have to close more of the gap. The wider the gap, the greater the need for visionary innovation.

With that in mind, part of the purpose of this book is to appeal to readers to become involved with the innovative financing wave. As the Landau Report mentioned in Chapter 2 showed, there are scores of ways to raise money by harnessing the power of markets and probably scores more that are still to be explored. The key will always be to distort the global economy as little as possible — its growth, after all, is the source of the wealth that can make a difference in poor countries.

The best way to reduce distortion is to make people *want* to play a part in the fight against poverty and disease. If your preference is to contribute — whether when you're buying an airline ticket, trading currency, or participating in any other activity — asking you to do so via a tax implies zero economic distortion. As an analogy, taxing your wages wouldn't discourage you from working if you actually *wanted* to pay the tax, presumably because you believed in the value of the things that your taxes would buy. This is why building solidarity is an essential ingredient for the success of innovative financing. But solidarity doesn't happen by itself; if it did, we might not be in this situation, with millions of people dying every year from treatable diseases. So UNITAID and the other innovative financing mechanisms must play a role in bringing people together, too.

MASSIVE GOOD. That simple phrase expresses, in two words, what UNITAID hopes to achieve as it looks toward the future. Massive good embodies the idea that huge numbers of people, by making slight changes in their daily lives, can make a huge difference in the lives of millions of poor and diseased people. It is also, as MassiveGood, the brand name under which the voluntary contribution reaches the individual consumer. And finally, MassiveGood is the name of the movement that will unite those who want to show that their solidarity can cross borders and oceans to touch their fellow human beings.

Even before the launch of the voluntary contribution, MassiveGood's Facebook page already had thousands of fans around the world. By the end of this year, it will have become a well-known brand encountered by air travelers in many countries when they book their tickets. Further into the future, it will link people in rich and poor countries in a way that treats both groups with equal dignity and transparency.

For givers, the story will not end after they check a box on a travel website as they're buying airline tickets. First, they will be able to track the medicine or equipment that they have helped to purchase as it makes its way from the factories where it is made to the towns and villages where it will save lives. Next, they will be able to stay abreast of UNITAID and the Millennium Foundation's activities and spending plans through e-mail updates and a website. In addition, Massive Good will help them to organize at a grassroots level. In rich countries, MassiveGood will encourage consumers and businesses to make the voluntary contribution and follow its results. In poor countries that receive aid, MassiveGood will encourage local people to monitor the delivery and implementation of medical treatments. Through an online nexus created by MassiveGood, these two groups will be able to interact, building greater ties of engagement and solidarity. Eventually, through its own social activism and through direct involvement in UNITAID and the Millennium Foundation, the MassiveGood community could play its own role in clos-

ing the gap, helping to turn the tide of the world's three dead-
liest infectious diseases.

In this way, a simple check box could do more than just
save lives, fight poverty, raise economic growth, and reduce
the likelihood of conflict in the future. It could also help to
build bridges between the rich and the poor, the comfortable
and the suffering, and the developed and the developing to an
unprecedented degree.

Chapter 6

The Future of Innovative Financing

A spirit of harmony can only survive if each of
us remembers, when bitterness and self-interest
seem to prevail, that we share a common destiny.
— BARBARA JORDAN

INNOVATIVE FINANCING is a young field, and it is a field born out of necessity. Perhaps, in the best of all possible worlds, people from around the world would already have asked their governments to deliver enough foreign aid to stop millions of senseless deaths from treatable diseases in poor countries. This has not happened, but the battle is not lost.

Innovative financing recognizes two important facts that will help to close the gap in funding for the fight against disease. First, that as a society we have not used or even invented all the tools that could help to raise money and control the epidemics. Second, that millions of people want to give more, to contribute more. The mission of innovative financing in the few years since its inception — UNITAID, the International

Finance Facility for Immunization, and Product (Red) all began operating in 2006 — has been to find those tools and to reach those people.

MassiveGood is not the first organization to collect checkbox donations for a cause; as we detailed in Chapter 4, eBay has given its users the chance to do this for millions of transactions. IFFIm is not the first organization to issue bonds for a cause; countries have been doing this for years to fund their wars. And Product (Red) is not the first organization to offer consumers the chance to make donations with purchases of specific products; the practice is so popular as to be classified as a marketing ploy. But together, these three organizations are the first to use these techniques to finance a single cause, taking advantage of market forces both to ensure their long-term funding and to make their spending more powerful. These organizations are truly innovative, and they are truly capable of saving millions of lives.

Because of their size and reach, they can also serve to alert potential contributors to urgent and important problems. Hundreds of smaller organizations would have fewer economies of scale in providing this informational service and might also lack the credibility of a large entity backed by governments and respected international groups. By providing a bridge between rich and poor countries, innovative financing can also highlight differences in the treatment of human beings, such as the vast gap in the treatment of pregnant women with HIV in the developed and developing worlds. In rich countries, mother-to-child transmission of HIV has been practically eliminated. In poor countries, it continues to occur in tens of thousands of cases every year, as pregnant women transmit death even as they give life — a fundamental and avoidable human injustice. By casting a spotlight on the spread of the big three epidemics, innovative financing mechanisms also show that these are diseases of inequality and not just biology or geography.

Clearly, the combination of official aid, innovative financing, and private charity does not necessarily represent the first or best solution in terms of helping poor countries to develop. The balance between the three contributors to the development effort is decided by politics as much as anything else, not by economic and social efficiency. Moreover, our current political models are not very good at preserving and improving social welfare in the world as a whole because they do not explicitly account for how the actions of one country might affect the destinies of others. As our difficulties in dealing with calamities such as climate change and genocide amply demonstrate, we have trouble coordinating our actions when no single country has sufficient incentive to solve the problem by itself. Yet innovative financing, by offering a channel for this coordination, can help to ensure the provision of so-called "global public goods" — universally beneficial things that everyone can enjoy — such as public health and a peaceful world.

In fact, European leaders recently proposed an innovative financing solution to combat the consequences of climate change: a tax on bank transactions whose proceeds would be directed, along with other sources of money, to the most direly affected developing countries. The organization that collects and dispenses the money could, like UNITAID, avoid any political affiliation and confine its investments to opportunities where the need, the science, and the bang for the buck align. Without independent organizations to coordinate and to be the face of these efforts, governments might be reluctant to come forward on their own. They might worry that other governments would benefit without doing their part, or that a donation might be construed as an implicit acknowledgment of responsibility for global warming.

The role of innovative financing is equally important in the private sector. Just as countries have a hard time coordinating to address global problems, companies have little incentive to spend the billions of dollars needed to develop drugs for people who, by themselves, can pay very little for them. This problem can be solved in two ways: first, by coordinating the resources and efforts of the companies themselves, as UNITAID is striving to do with its new patent pool, and second, through redistribution of global wealth.

Innovative financing provides an extra, credible mechanism of redistribution for citizens who might like their governments to give more official aid but who find themselves in a minority. This mechanism is especially important in strongly capitalist countries where the tax-and-transfer systems offer little scope for redistribution of global wealth. But nothing is inconsistent with capitalism and innovative financing: If citizens of these countries want to give money to well-organized and well-managed programs to benefit the developing world, their governments should not stand in the way. By giving their citizens more ways to do what they want with their money, these countries would be enhancing their citizens' well-being by expanding their freedom of choice.

Yet while voluntary contributions are free of economic distortions and avoid the political controversies associated with taxes, they do have one drawback: a free rider problem. Every dollar donated to fight the big three infectious diseases benefits *every* citizen in the world, not just those who contribute, by prolonging lives, enhancing global economic growth, and reducing the potential for instability in the developing world. Millions of people might choose to make a voluntary contribution through MassiveGood, but millions of people in the same socioeconomic group probably won't — and yet they will all enjoy the same benefits as more people get the treatments they need. If it becomes common knowledge that, say, only one in ten air travelers pays the voluntary contribution, will even that minority decide that they're fed up with subsidizing their fellow consumers? Or, even worse, will governments take the low rate of participation as a negative verdict on foreign aid in general? We think that the answer is no — that people give because they want to help the world solve its problems. But to guarantee the future of innovative financing, its stewards will have to consider these issues as well.

As a whole, the innovative financing mechanisms have in their short lives mobilized close to two-and-a-half billion dollars in supplementary financing for global health programs, contributing to, among other achievements, the vaccination of one hundred million children and the guaranteed treatment of HIV/AIDS for a new cohort of one hundred thousand children every year, encompassing three out of four children who receive antiretroviral treatment in the developing world. The sum may sound huge and the achievements great, but they represent only part of the shortfall that innovative financing hopes to eliminate. The pursuit of the Millennium Development Goals has shown just how wide the gap in funding is between official aid and the amounts of money needed to turn the tide against poverty, disease, and damage to the environment: perhaps tens of billions of dollars per year.

In the future, four families of innovative financing mechanisms will continue to grow and develop: small taxes assessed on globalized activities, such as airline tickets and currency transactions; methods of making upfront investments using the financial markets and government guarantees or promises, such as the International Finance Facility for Immunization (which borrows from the markets using bonds to place bulk orders for vaccines) and the Advance Market Commitment (which uses promises of future demand to lower prices and raise production of drugs); market mechanisms such as the auctions for tradable pollution permits, whose proceeds might go to global causes; and facilities for channeling direct contributions from the private sector through governments and international groups, such as MassiveGood and Product (Red).

Through the Leading Group on Innovative Financing for Development, governments are exploring new frontiers both in types of mechanisms and the causes for which they can be used. New initiatives include reducing the costs attached to remittances sent by migrant workers to their friends and family in developing countries. At present, the cost stands at roughly 10 percent of the amount sent, on average. Led by the Italian government, a new project will try to reduce that share to 5 percent within five years, in part by setting up national websites for remittances that will direct visitors to the least expensive ways of sending money to their countries — essentially a buyers' markets for remittance services. Another initiative will try to collect a small tax on information technology procurement contracts in rich countries to fund projects that close the digital divide in poor countries.

Innovative financing will grow even more by developing new ways of raising money and new ways of spending it. The priority for raising money will always be to supplement official aid by harnessing the power of markets. The best way to do that will be to isolate opportunities that, like MassiveGood, fit these fundamental criteria:

1. The funds are collected from a large base: many consumers, many transactions, or both.

2. The funds are collected in a way that minimally distorts the global economy.

3. The base for fund-raising can easily be accessed through a small number of gatekeepers.

4. The base for fund-raising includes more of the global economy's haves than have-nots.

MassiveGood's voluntary contribution fits these criteria because the airline ticket market is enormous and international; voluntary contributions do not distort the market because they provide only a further option for spending money; the three reservations systems — Amadeus, Sabre, and Travelport — cover the vast majority of transactions; and airline tickets are generally purchased by people who, in global terms, are quite well-off.

What other mechanisms might fit these criteria? In many large markets, most of the transactions are accessible through a limited number of gatekeepers or clearinghouses. The Landau Report — the document that led to UNITAID's creation — identified markets for arms, carbon credits, financial transactions, and international shipping. But these lack one thing that the market for airline tickets has: They are not populated primarily by individual consumers, but rather by businesses.

This difference is important, because the level of international aid should, when all is said and done, correspond to popular preferences. By placing a tax on businesses or asking them to make voluntary contributions, individuals would be delegating the decision about aid to their governments and to shareholders and managers of companies. Given the reluctance of politicians to institute new taxes and the profit motive that drives most businesses, the level of aid set by governments and corporate leaders might be lower than individuals would prefer.

Mechanisms that raise funds from businesses could still be an important component of the fight against poverty, privation, and disease. But the most effective mechanisms may be those that go straight to consumers, such as MassiveGood and Product (Red). In this area, the options are more varied and even esoteric. For starters, innovating financing groups seeking new markets could focus on retail outlets with a high volume of transactions, such as Amazon.com. Even if not every purchase on Amazon.com costs as much as an airline ticket, a check box might still raise substantial revenue by approaching millions of people directly and simply.

Another possibility is a global lottery. Lotteries are popular, and a substantial share of their revenue can be separated from the prize money without diminishing the public's interest. Typical payouts in American lotteries amount to just two-thirds of the money collected from ticket sales. Lotteries are completely voluntary, and a global lottery would have an enormous consumer base. As the Landau Report points out, another advantage is that several lotteries could be created for different causes, allowing consumers to choose where they put their money. Lotteries are not progressive, however; they are popular in poor countries as well as rich ones, and poor people spend a higher percentage of their income on lottery tickets than rich people.

A more precisely directed strategy might target people who are among the greatest beneficiaries of globalization:

those who, as consumers, buy products that are either imported or made using imported goods and services. A tiny tariff or voluntary contribution might be assessed on imported items costing one thousand dollars or more, from clothes washers to cars. These measures could not be considered protectionist if they were assessed globally. A tariff would hardly be large enough to discourage people from buying imports — an important consideration especially if the imports are coming from developing countries — and a voluntary contribution would, of course, have no distorting effect whatsoever.

A program like this would have a huge potential for fundraising. In the crisis year of 2008, the United States alone imported $126 billion worth of passenger cars. Even if some categories of vehicles were exempted, a 0.01 percent tax — 1¢ on every $100 — might have collected about $10 million. As an alternative, a check box to donate $10 per vehicle might also have raised a substantial sum. According to the U.S. Department of Energy, the average price of an imported car is about $30,000, so imports amounted to about 4.2 million cars. If a quarter of buyers had made the voluntary contribution, the collections would have amounted to about $10 million. And that's just for one market, in one country.

More opportunities exist to use the financial markets as a pathway for innovative financing. One is to combine the methods of microcredit with those of existing mechanisms such as the International Finance Facility for Immunization. A possible model is the online charity Kiva, which has shown that people are willing to make small, zero-interest loans to give individual borrowers in the developing world enough liquidity to make modest investments that improve their standards of living. An innovative financing mechanism might set up a clearinghouse for these microloans similar to Kiva's, but rather than dispensing the money directly to individuals, it could bundle the money to make big game-changing investments in health, education, or other key areas. Countries would receive the benefits of these investments as long as they promised to pay back the principal of the loans over time. This mechanism would mirror some aspects of official aid, but it would also differ in several important ways. One, its funds would come from a vast group of individual lenders. Two, the funds would be only for specific types of programs known to the lenders (for example, to buy vaccines or schoolbooks). And three, a central organization would determine where and how to invest for maximum effect. The crucial part would be to choose forms of aid that would improve the participating countries' economic futures, so that they could easily pay back the loans.

This kind of mechanism could be extremely powerful, because it adds financial leverage to small donations. When people make zero-interest loans through organizations such as Kiva, they are actually making a combination of a loan and a donation; the donation is the foregone interest that they could have received in the regular financial markets. Take the example of a zero-interest loan for fifty dollars to be paid back after five years. Let's say that this loan might normally have carried an interest rate of 10 percent, given the time period and risk of default. In today's dollars, those interest payments would be worth about twenty-three dollars. By forgoing interest, the lender thus makes a donation of twenty-three dollars. But unlike a regular charitable gift of twenty-three dollars, this loan makes fifty dollars available right away for an upfront investment that could accelerate the development of a poor country. In this way, the mechanism would use one of the fundamental techniques of the financial markets — leverage — to more than double the power of a small donation.

In the meantime, one of the original ideas from the Landau Report, a tax on transactions in the financial markets, may be gaining new momentum. In September 2009, Nicolas Sarkozy, now France's president, put the tax back on the world agenda at the meeting of the G-20 economic powers in Pittsburgh. The original motivation for the tax as proposed by the economist James Tobin — to reduce speculation and sharp swings in the markets — had become more attractive in the wake of the financial crisis. Thanks to the continuing dialogue on innovative financing and the constant advocacy of people such as David Hillman from the Stamp Out Poverty campaign in the United Kingdom, it was virtually implicit that the proceeds of any tax would go to global causes including the Millennium Development Goals. This time, however, there was a twist. A more modest yet much more feasible plan was being conceived as an alternative to the original idea: taxing the transactions between the world's central banks at the Bank for International Settlements (BIS).

The BIS essentially acts as a central bank for central banks. Just as the Federal Reserve allows commercial banks to lend reserves to each other so they can balance their risks and meet their overnight cash requirements, the BIS allows the world's central banks to trade reserves of gold and currencies to achieve their own portfolio goals. These trades can amount to hundreds of billions of dollars every working day. To raise one million dollars a day from transactions worth, say, one hundred billion dollars requires a tax rate of just 0.001 percent, equivalent to one one-hundred-thousandth of the value of the transactions. And the best part is that the BIS already levies a tiny tax on these transactions to finance its own operations, so the machinery to collect the money is already in place.

Even such a small tax would raise hundreds of millions of dollars every year, enough to treat hundreds of thousands of children with HIV/AIDS, or to cure hundreds of thousands of adults of tuberculosis, or to buy tens of millions of antimalaria bednets and pills. Its effects could be just as powerful as the voluntary contribution for travelers.

THE OTHER CHALLENGE going forward is to find new kinds of innovative spending. Clearly, the advantage of the innovative financing mechanisms is their ability to gather together large amounts of money in a short time, and the way to exploit that advantage is to use the money where its sheer bulk can make a difference. These opportunities will appear when at least one of the following criteria is met:

1. The money is used to buy something that has economies of scale in its production and can usefully be distributed from a central source.

2. The money is used to pay for something that requires a significant upfront investment.

3. The money is used to initiate a virtuous circle in the provision of some good or service, such as raising demand to gain economies of scale, which in turn lowers prices and leads to more demand.

But even before seeking one or more of these basic criteria, we might want to consider another group of criteria for spending that is based on current ideas about economic development.

Mainstream thinking has changed substantially since the era when economic experts thought that they could turn poor countries into rich ones by throwing money at them indiscriminately. The thinking now disfavors huge spending programs in many cases, on the basis of three issues. The first is who will receive the money; after so many years of seeing billions of dollars of aid siphoned away by corrupt elites, aid organizations and governments have become more careful. The World Bank, for example, now makes the consideration of corruption a central part of its lending decisions. The second is whether there are actually enough useful projects to use the money productively; this issue, usually called "absorptive capacity," is of particular concern in very poor countries unused to enormous inflows of capital. To see the importance of this issue, one only has to examine poor countries with enormous oil wealth, where the money is often either wasted (as in Nigeria, for decades) or saved (as in Timor-Leste, more recently) because of a lack of productive opportunities. The third is whether the projects will yield the right kind of results for the specific challenges facing a given country; one-size-fits-all solutions such as the package of pro-market policies once known as the "Washington Consensus" have, by and large, fallen by the wayside. More tailored development plans are now in vogue, such as the Millennium Villages Project, in which small communities receive financial and technical assistance from outside but identify and solve problems on their own.

UNITAID's spending priorities fit both sets of criteria. For example, generic drugs have economies of scale in their production (so big orders can lower their prices), and they can also be distributed centrally through credible organizations such as UNICEF and the Clinton HIV/AIDS initiative; the creation of pediatric doses and the transformation of syrups into pills require upfront investment in research and development; and the creation of improved public health systems in poor countries would help to create a cycle of better health, less conflict, and more stable economic growth.

Moreover, because UNITAID provides funding for in-kind donations of lifesaving drugs that go only to people who really need them, the questions of absorptive capacity and specificity are largely irrelevant. Saving a life has an unambiguously positive effect in social and economic terms. It does require paying the upfront cost of treatment — which is why the existing mechanisms try to raise such large sums so quickly — but it unlocks a long stream of benefits that stretch far into the future.

These are not the only investments that might fit one or more of the criteria, however. One can imagine applying them to other fields, such as education. At the moment, school supplies from pencils to laptops can be difficult to obtain in poor countries. Centralized purchasing and distribution could reduce prices substantially. In fact, globally centralized spending might add further economies of scale to those that already exist, for example, in the One Laptop Per Child program, which provides hundreds of thousands of laptops to children in developing countries at a cost of $150 to $200 per computer. Governments place large orders, but people can donate laptops on an individual basis as well. If one central purchaser bought the laptops and then sold them back to governments and other buyers, however, the cost might be brought down even further, perhaps to the program's initial target of $100.

Many developing countries also suffer from a lack of financing for higher education, so it is hard for poor people to go to college. Under these conditions, it is difficult to create income mobility or a professional middle class, and the distribution of wealth may remain polarized even as a country is growing. Funding university scholarships for children of poor families can break that status quo and begin a virtuous circle of higher educational attainment and higher incomes from generation to generation. In addition, the selection and financing of students may best be achieved by large organizations that can take advantage of economies of scale.

Innovative financing mechanisms will still exist after the tide is turned against the major epidemics (should we be fortunate enough to see that day). Even now, innovative financing mechanisms are being considered as a means of solving other problems. They have the potential to provide a framework for confronting global challenges that governments have tried and failed to take on by themselves, such as how to help refugees of conflict start new lives and how to clean up polluted rivers and seas whose waters are shared by several countries.

IN ADDITION to creating solidarity between rich and poor individuals, innovative financing may also be able to point the way forward for cooperation between countries as an adjunct to their existing economic and political systems. The patent pool provides a blueprint for this kind of cooperation, breaking down the traditional barriers between competing companies and the governments on whose legal protections they rely. Initiatives such as the patent pool offer the prospect of doing something that no organizations have accomplished in the past: coordinating the resources of governments, private companies, charitable foundations, and individuals to take on specific goals in international development, in a setting relatively free from political expediencies.

Another potential area for cooperation is in regulating markets with harmful side effects through corrective taxes. In many markets, buyers and sellers incur costs to society above and beyond the costs and benefits to themselves. These markets include anything whose production or consumption pollutes the environment, increases health risks, reduces opportunities, or otherwise detracts from other people's well-being, such as cigarettes (which can annoy and sicken the people around the user), gasoline (whose consumption pollutes the air), and fatty food (which leads to higher medical care costs borne by taxpayers). Quite a few of these markets are already taxed, the logic being that a tax discourages buyers and sellers and brings the number of transactions down to a more socially optimal level. Some of these markets are not taxed, though, and others could still be taxed in a more economically efficient way. If groups of countries were to sign on to these corrective taxes and channel the proceeds to good causes, they could help to improve social welfare in two ways at the same time.

The Leading Group is also exploring ways in which innovative financing can act as a buffer in times of economic volatility and crisis. By tapping markets that react less strongly to fluctuations than the economy as a whole, such as airline tickets, innovative financing mechanisms can provide a stable source of funding for international aid at a time when government revenues and other private donations may lag. In addition, the capacity of innovative financing mechanisms to raise large sums of money in short periods of time means that they can smooth their spending on aid projects over the long term, rather than engaging in the kind of money-in, money-out funding practices of politically controlled organizations. This situation implies what economists would call a "moral hazard" problem, however. Knowing that innovative financing could provide a cushion, other donors might deliberately lower their level of funding, regardless of the economic circumstances, creating a net drop in aid.

In the best-case scenario, innovative financing will have the opposite effect. By bringing urgent global problems to the attention of the public, the innovative financing mechanisms might change citizens' preferences and lead them to lobby their governments for more official aid as well. The same could be true for smaller aid organizations that might feel threatened by the fund-raising capacity of the innovative financing mechanisms; if the mechanisms help to highlight their causes, they might actually receive more donations.

GOING FORWARD, one key question will be whether innovative financing mechanisms will fall short of their full potential because of political differences between countries. The implementation of the airline ticket tax has been idiosyncratic, as has the willingness of countries to participate in IFFIm, AMC, and other mechanisms. The possible reasons for countries not to join are numerous: Their own debts might make spending on foreigners politically unfeasible; an unstable economic cycle might make it too difficult to commit to steady support of an innovative financing mechanism; their people may believe that they already send enough money for international causes; or they may simply have other political priorities taking up all their legislative time.

Those challenges, however, can be turned into opportunities. After all, the impetus for the voluntary contribution with airline ticket sales was the refusal of the United States government to consider the airline ticket tax. The voluntary contribution deals with several of the issues just listed simultaneously: It requires no government spending, it is optional for consumers, and its implementation depends entirely on the private sector.

Indeed, the voluntary contribution demonstrates that the same forces that are pushing forward the current wave of globalization can be exploited to make innovative financing more powerful. The integration of the global economy, through formal means such as trade agreements and informal means such as the Internet, has created commercial pathways between countries that did not previously exist. These pathways allow mechanisms such as innovative financing to access and harness new markets without needing an official invitation.

Innovative financing mechanisms that work through the private sector have one more advantage: They will grow in countries that grow. Not all the economic gains from globalization have been concentrated in rich countries; many poor countries, including giants such as China and India, have also seen hundreds of millions of people escape from poverty as foreign investment has flowed in and exports have flowed out. In places like these, more and more consumers will begin to encounter the innovative financing mechanisms in their daily lives, and they will have a chance to show their solidarity with the less fortunate as well, regardless of whether their governments are ready to start sending official aid abroad.

As INNOVATIVE FINANCING mechanisms proliferate, some broader risks will begin to emerge. One will have to do with the management and goals of innovative financing mechanisms. Two sets of stakeholders must always be represented in their leadership: the countries and people who are supposed to be helped, and the countries and people who are supplying most of the funding. If either group becomes too powerful in a given innovative financing mechanism, the results could significantly reduce its effectiveness. For instance, a board dominated by the givers might favor pet projects rather than those truly needed by developing countries, or might become too wound up in the selection of new projects or other bureaucratic processes to be able to deliver aid where needed in a timely fashion. Alternatively, a board dominated by representatives from developing countries might be vulnerable to shifts in the political winds; the election of corrupt leaders could lead to funds being channeled to their supporters rather than to the neediest citizens, or worse.

Either outcome would present an additional risk, namely that the failure of one innovative financing mechanism would stain the reputation of them all. This is a particularly worrying prospect now, in the early days of innovative financing, because its identity as a class of aid organizations has not been fully established in the mind of the public. First impressions count, and if the first impression for potential donors is a scandal in the pages of a newspaper, innovative financing will have a tough time forging a good reputation.

To head off these risks, the creation of a supervisory authority for innovative financing mechanisms — even a self-regulating one based on the I-8 mentioned previously — might be a useful step. At the very least, such an authority could provide a Good Housekeeping Seal of Approval for new innovative financing mechanisms that meet the criteria discussed previously for economic effectiveness and solid governance. It would be important that the various mechanisms maintained their independence, because their commitment to different causes would likely to be a key component of their success. But to have an industry body that exists for most types of companies that must gain the public's trust would surely help all the mechanisms reach their full potential to help those in need.

THAT TRUST WILL HELP to confirm innovative financing as a crucial component of the aid equation, alongside government assistance and private charities. As we said earlier, in the best of all possible worlds, innovative financing mechanisms might not be necessary. But because of the political and economic realities we face, they could and should play an important role in the struggle to save millions of lives.

We believe that the world will benefit enormously from the expansion of innovative financing mechanisms, providing they coordinate their efforts to maximize their effectiveness and complement other sources of aid. As we wait for more mechanisms to emerge and engage with people around the world, UNITAID and the Millennium Foundation will continue to seek new sources of innovative financing and new kinds of innovative spending. MassiveGood will be at the forefront, as its brand gains the recognition and trust of consumers and its social network links more and more people in rich and poor countries. It will be the capstone to a peaceful but revolutionary effort to eliminate one of the greatest humanitarian tragedies of our time. We hope that you, our reader, will join us in this effort.

Tables

TABLE 1. Innovative Financing: Members of UNITAID and Funds Contributed (* = pending)

Country or Donor	Date Inducted	Contribution Type	Amount Collected
Brazil	September 2006	Cash contribution	$38,295,000
Chile	September 2006	Airline ticket tax	13,333,000
France	September 2006	Airline ticket tax	625,203,000
Norway	September 2006	Carbon dioxide tax	67,957,000
United Kingdom	September 2006	Cash contribution	102,644,000
Benin	February 2007	Airline ticket tax	*
Burkina Faso	February 2007	Airline ticket tax	*
Cameroon	February 2007		
Central African Republic	February 2007		
Congo	February 2007	Airline ticket tax	*
Côte d'Ivoire	February 2007	Airline ticket tax	*
Gabon	February 2007		
Liberia	February 2007		
Madagascar	February 2007	Airline ticket tax	*
Mali	February 2007	Airline ticket tax	*
Mauritius	February 2007	Airline ticket tax	3,991,000
Morocco	February 2007		
Namibia	February 2007		
Niger	February 2007	Airline ticket tax	304,000

(*continues*)

TABLE 1. (*continued*)

Country or Donor	Date Inducted	Contribution Type	Amount Collected
Sao Tome and Principe	February 2007		
Senegal	February 2007		
South Africa	February 2007		
Togo	February 2007		
Spain	May 2007	Cash contribution	63,856,000
Guinea	August 2007	Airline ticket tax	99,000
South Korea	December 2007	Airline ticket tax	14,000,000
Luxembourg	December 2008	Cash contribution	734,000
Cyprus	December 2009	Cash contribution	587,000
Gates Foundation	Founding board member	Cash contribution	20,000,000

TABLE 2. Innovative Spending: UNITAID Projects and Funds Disbursed

Project Name	Timeframe	Disbursements through 2009	Results
Pediatric antiretrovirals	2006–2009	$145,963,748	265,000 children in treatment; drugs reformatted; prices cut by 60 percent
Prevention of mother-to-child HIV transmission	2007–2010	41,363,706	3,900,000 women tested for HIV; 260,000 receiving antiretrovirals; 242,000 tested for anemia
Second-line antiretrovirals	2007–2009	145,468,038	58,000 patients on second-line drugs; 114,000 on first-line drugs
ESTHERAID training and capacity building	2008–2011	451,626	Implemented in five countries
Pediatric tuberculosis	2006–2011	9,624,301	385,000 treatments; first-ever pediatric drug qualified for use
First-line antituberculosis treatments	2007–2008	26,840,725	787,000 treatments; three drugs qualified; prices cut
Multiple-drug-resistant tuberculosis	2007–2011	54,429,571	Annual quota for available doses quadrupled; prices cut by 80 percent
Antimalarial drug supply and scale-up	2008–2011	53,682,535	29.7 million drug courses delivered; production raised

Notes

CHAPTER ONE

2   "Consider the death tolls . . ." table — "China earth-
quake toll rises to 68,109," Xinhua News Service (May 28,
2008); Burnham, Gilbert et al., *The Human Cost of the War in
Iraq: A Mortality Study, 2002–2006,* MIT Center for International Studies (2006); "Asia's tsunami death toll soars," BBC
News (January 20, 2005); Asiimwe, Arthur, "Rwanda census
puts genocide death toll at 937,000," Reuters (April 4,
2004); "The CGP, 1994–2008," Yale University Cambodian
Genocide Project, via www.yale.edu/cgp/; World Health
Organization, *Fact Sheets,* No. 310 (November 2008).

4   "Since 1970, the United Nations has asked . . ." — "The
0.7% target: An in-depth look," *United Nations Millennium
Project* (2006) via www.unmillenniumproject.org.

6   "But no single infectious disease causes as many
deaths . . ." — World Health Organization, *Global Burden of
Disease* (2004).

6   ". . . these three diseases caused one in eight of all deaths . . ." — World Health Organization, *Fact Sheets*, No. 310 (November 2008).

7   "Moreover, the three diseases interact." — from discussions with Candice Kwan M.D. of the New York University Medical Center; Tuberculosis Coalition for Technical Assistance, *International Standards for Tuberculosis Care* (2006); and Steketee, Richard, "Interactions of HIV and Malaria," *Program Abstracts of the Conference on Retroviruses and Opportunistic Infections*, No. 143 (2004).

7   "The overall prevalence rate could be as high as . . ." — Wu, Xueqiong et al., "Latent tuberculosis infection amongst new recruits to the Chinese army: Comparison of ELISPOT assay and tuberculin skin test," *Clinica Chimica Acta*, Vol. 405, No. 1–2 (July 2009), pp. 110–113 and Bennett, Diane E. et al., "Prevalence of Tuberculosis Infection in the United States Population: The National Health and Nutrition Examination Survey, 1999–2000," *American Journal of Respiratory and Critical Care Medicine*, Vol. 177 (2008), pp. 348–355.

8   "Worldwide, the mortality rate for heart disease . . ." — World Health Organization, *World Health Statistics* (2009).

8   "Instead of dying at seven . . ." — World Health Organization, *Life Tables for WHO Member States*, "Burkina Faso" (2006).

9   ". . . people living in three-quarters of the country . . ."
— The Global Fund to Fight AIDS, Tuberculosis and Malaria,
grant proposal submitted by Guatemala for fourth round of
funding (January 10, 2004).

9   "Per capita income in Guatemala . . ." — Central Intelligence Agency, *The World Factbook 2009,* www.cia.gov/
library/publications/the-world-factbook/index.html.

10   "About $6 for a full course . . ." — Global Malaria
Partnership, "Roll Back Malaria: Key Facts," www.rollback-
malaria.org/keyfacts.html.

10   "From 1969 to 2009, Warren Buffett, perhaps the
world's most famous investor . . ." — Buffett's wealth in
1969: Hagstrom, Robert G., *The Warren Buffett Way* (Wiley,
1994); Buffett's wealth in 2009: Miller, Matthew and Duncan
Greenberg, "The Richest People in America," *Forbes* (September 30, 2009); figure adjusted for inflation using statistics
from the U.S. Bureau of Labor Statistics.

10   ". . . such as the rape of virgin girls . . ." — "Child rape
survivor saves 'virgin myth' victims," *CNN.com* (October 1,
2009).

10   "As early as 1987, a report . . ." — Garrett, Laurie,
"HIV and National Security: Where Are the Links?" (Council
on Foreign Relations, 2005).

10 "One academic study using data from developing countries . . ." — Peterson, Susan and Stephen M. Shellman, "AIDS and Violent Conflict: The Indirect Effects of Disease on National Security," *Institute for the Theory and Practice of International Relations Working Paper Series* (2006).

11 "Other recent research by Andrew Price-Smith . . ." — Price-Smith, Andrew T., *Contagion and Chaos: Disease, Ecology, and National Security in the Era of Globalization* (MIT Press, 2009).

11 "As Tandja Mamadou, Niger's president, said . . ." — this paragraph draws on the personal conversations and experiences of Philippe Douste-Blazy.

13 "In 2007, wealthy countries committed $118 billion . . ." — Organization for Economic Cooperation and Development, *DAC5 Official Bilateral Commitments by Sector* (April 2009).

13 "At the beginning of 2007 . . ." — World Health Organization, "Towards universal access: scaling up priority HIV/AIDS interventions in the health sector: progress report" (April 2007) [and cost figures from the same source].

CHAPTER TWO

16 ". . . Chirac encouraged his fellow heads of state . . ." — Bonta, Steve, "New push for global taxes," *The New American,* Vol. 18, No. 8 (April 22, 2002).

19 "Even Chirac himself called the ideas . . ." — Lee, Matthew, "France, Brazil lead charge for new global anti-poverty campaign," *Agence France Presse* (September 20, 2004).

19 "Tony Fratto, a spokesman for the Treasury . . ." — Sparshott, Jeffrey, "World leaders mull French call for $10 billion AIDS tax," *The Washington Times* (January 28, 2005).

19 "But in late March 2005 . . ." — "Chirac urges airline tax by end of year to help Africa," *Agence France Presse* (March 28, 2005).

20 "Two-thirds of the hotel nights . . ." — data for 2005 from the French ministry of tourism, published September 2006.

CHAPTER THREE

46 "Many of the retailers have never sold . . ." — this and other facts in this section come from private conversations with people involved with the project and its evaluation.

51   "During the recent global economic crisis . . ." — Blair, Elizabeth, "Assessing Impact of Financial Crisis on Nonprofits," *National Public Radio* (September 30, 2008); "Financial crisis creating 'perfect storm' for charity organizations," *CBC News* (November 10, 2008); Jamieson, Alastair, "Charity donations hit by financial crisis," *The Daily Telegraph* (November 8, 2008).

53   "Together, these companies control the lion's share . . ." — Starkov, Max, "Online Travel Agencies (OTAs): Will They Survive the Removal of Airline Ticket Booking Fees?" *Hospitality E-Business Strategies Internet Marketing Blog* (July 8, 2009).

CHAPTER FOUR

63   "Much less uncertainty exists about public health . . ." — see, for example, the discussion in Banerjee, Abhijit, *Making Aid Work* (MIT Press, 2007).

73   ". . . Americans planning for retirement, for example . . ." — Poterba, James M., Steven F. Venti and David A. Wise, "How Retirement Saving Programs Increase Saving," *Journal of Economic Perspectives,* Vol. 10, No. 4 (Fall 1996), pp. 91–112.

75   "An analysis of the breakfast cereal industry . . ." — Schmalensee, Richard, "Entry Deterrence in the Ready-to-Eat

Breakfast Cereal Industry," *Bell Journal of Economics,* Vol. 9, No. 2 (Autumn 1978), pp. 305–327.

78   ". . . perhaps, as one dean suggested, air conditioning . . ." — Anonymous, "Greater Expectations: FAS enhances teaching, learning, and scholarship," *The Harvard Gazette* (January 29, 1998); the article also mentions that fund-raising for libraries had reached less than half its goal of $67 million, though a previous article in the same publication ("Articulating, Then Answering, Library's Needs," September 18, 1997) had stated that the goal was $78 million.

80   ". . . elicited some worried reactions . . ." — according to an interview with Khalil Elouardighi on July 22, 2009.

CHAPTER FIVE

83   "If the top fifty countries by purchases . . ." — Douste-Blazy, Philippe, UNITAID presentation to the WHO Expert Group on Innovative Financing (Geneva, January 13, 2009); additional information from private conversations.

85   "The Toshiba/Warner discs could store more data . . ." — Pollack, Andrew, "Big makers agree on single format for multi-use disk," *The New York Times* (September 16, 1995).

86   "The World Trade Organization's arcane rules . . ." —

Mayne, Ruth, "The recent agreement on WTO patent rules and access to medicines: a flawed deal?" *The Courier ACP-EU,* No. 201 (November–December 2003).

90   ". . . that seemingly gigantic figure is tiny . . ." — U.S. Centers for Disease Control, "Malaria: Topic Home" via www.cdc.gov/malaria.

97   "In fact, European leaders recently proposed . . ." — Charter, David, Rory Watson and Philippe Naughton, "Gordon Brown and Nicolas Sarkozy: banks should pay for climate change," The Times (December 11, 2009).

103   "Typical payouts in American lotteries . . ." — Quint, Michael, "New York Lottery Shuns Treasuries in Bid for Riskier Investment," Bloomberg News (February 10, 2009).

103   ". . . poor people spend a higher percentage of their income . . ." — Clotfelter, Charles T., "Do Lotteries Hurt the Poor? Well, Yes and No," summary of testimony before the North Carolina House Select Committee on a State Lottery (April 19, 2000).

104   "In the crisis year of 2008, the United States alone . . ."

— statistics from the U.S. Department of Commerce, Bureau of Economic Analysis.

104 "According to the U.S. Department of Energy . . ." — U.S. Department of Energy, "Fact of the Week, Fact #520" (May 26, 2008) via www.eere.energy.gov.

106 ". . . Nicolas Sarkozy, now France's president, put the tax back . . ." — "Sarkozy to press for 'Tobin Tax,'" *BBC News* (September 19, 2009).

108 "The World Bank, for example, now makes the consideration . . ." — The World Bank Group, "Corruption: How the World Bank Fights Corruption," via www.worldbank.org (February 2005).

109 "To see the importance of this issue . . ." — Altman, Daniel, *Connected: 24 Hours in the Global Economy* (Farrar, Straus and Giroux, 2007).

Further Reading

ENGLISH

Clinton, William J. and Philippe Douste-Blazy, "Keep the Promise," *International Herald Tribune* (January 3, 2009)

Douste-Blazy, Philippe, "A Tiny Tax Could Do a World of Good," *The New York Times* (September 24, 2009)

Gumbel, Peter, "New Airline-Ticket Tax to Aid the Developing World," *TIME* (September 18, 2009)

Strom, Stephanie, "Travelers' Fee Can Help Fight Diseases," *The New York Times* (September 23, 2009)

FRENCH

Clinton, William J. and Philippe Douste-Blazy, "Le tiers-monde peut-il survivre à la crise?" *Le Figaro* (March 6, 2009)

Gates, Bill, "Unitaid, une exemplaire contribution française pour sauver des vies dans le monde," *Le Figaro* (February 25, 2008)

Acknowledgments

Philippe Douste-Blazy thanks presidents Jacques Chirac of France, Luiz Inácio Lula da Silva of Brazil, and Ricardo Lagos of Chile, who were the first to propose innovative financing mechanisms for development; Ban-Ki Moon, secretary-general of the United Nations, for his personal involvement in the realization of the Millennium Development Goals for health; Margaret Chan, director-general of the World Health Organization, for her help in the day-to-day running of UNITAID; Philippe Duneton, Jorge Bermudez, Elizabeth Hoff, and the entire UNITAID team, who were committed from the beginning and opened the way forward; Jean Dussourd, for his pivotal involvement in the birth of UNITAID, along with Sandrine Boucher and Aurélien Lechevallier; Bernard Salomé and the team at the Millennium Foundation for having put the voluntary contribution in place so quickly; all the board members who followed me since the start of this adventure, particularly the members from France, without whom this adventure would neither have begun nor continued; the representatives of both the nongovernmental organizations — in particular Khalil Elouardighi, for his determination, his rigor, and his advice — and the patient organizations; Jean-François Rial, Philippe Chérèque, and all the representatives of private companies without whom the "first world citizens' voluntary solidarity contribution" never would have seen the light of day; and Laurence Thurion for her invaluable day-to-day assistance.

Daniel Altman thanks Philippe Douste-Blazy, Laurence Thurion, Jean-François Rial, Khalil Elouardighi, Bernard Salomé, Philippe Duneton, and Elizabeth Hoff for their generosity with their time. Jim Andreoni provided a useful viewpoint from academic economics. Candice Kwan shared her expertise on infectious diseases. Larry Weissman provided invaluable service as the agent for this book, and Clive Priddle and the excellent team at PublicAffairs made it a reality. Friends and family, as always, provided moral support.

Both authors also thank **President Bill Clinton** for the constancy and depth of his support, both for UNITAID and for this book.

All errors are our own.

Index

PublicAffairs is a publishing house founded in 1997. It is a tribute to the standards, values, and flair of three persons who have served as mentors to countless reporters, writers, editors, and book people of all kinds, including me.

I. F. Stone, proprietor of *I. F. Stone's Weekly,* combined a commitment to the First Amendment with entrepreneurial zeal and reporting skill and became one of the great independent journalists in American history. At the age of eighty, Izzy published *The Trial of Socrates,* which was a national bestseller. He wrote the book after he taught himself ancient Greek.

Benjamin C. Bradlee was for nearly thirty years the charismatic editorial leader of *The Washington Post*. It was Ben who gave the *Post* the range and courage to pursue such historic issues as Watergate. He supported his reporters with a tenacity that made them fearless, and it is no accident that so many became authors of influential, best-selling books.

Robert L. Bernstein, the chief executive of Random House for more than a quarter century, guided one of the nation's premier publishing houses. Bob was personally responsible for many books of political dissent and argument that challenged tyranny around the globe. He is also the founder and was the longtime chair of Human Rights Watch, one of the most respected human rights organizations in the world.

.   .   .

For fifty years, the banner of Public Affairs Press was carried by its owner Morris B. Schnapper, who published Gandhi, Nasser, Toynbee, Truman, and about 1,500 other authors. In 1983 Schnapper was described by *The Washington Post* as "a redoubtable gadfly." His legacy will endure in the books to come.

Peter Osnos, *Founder and Editor-at-Large*